GIVE ME BACK MY TIME

A FATHER'S HEARTFELT CONVERSATION WITH HIS DAUGHTER

SAPTARSHI SANKAR CHAKRABARTI

Copyright © SAPTARSHI SANKAR CHAKRABARTI
All Rights Reserved.

This book has been self-published with all reasonable efforts taken to make the material error-free by the author. No part of this book shall be used, reproduced in any manner whatsoever without written permission from the author, except in the case of brief quotations embodied in critical articles and reviews.

The Author of this book is solely responsible and liable for its content including but not limited to the views, representations, descriptions, statements, information, opinions and references ["Content"]. The Content of this book shall not constitute or be construed or deemed to reflect the opinion or expression of the Publisher or Editor. Neither the Publisher nor Editor endorse or approve the Content of this book or guarantee the reliability, accuracy or completeness of the Content published herein and do not make any representations or warranties of any kind, express or implied, including but not limited to the implied warranties of merchantability, fitness for a particular purpose. The Publisher and Editor shall not be liable whatsoever for any errors, omissions, whether such errors or omissions result from negligence, accident, or any other cause or claims for loss or damages of any kind, including without limitation, indirect or consequential loss or damage arising out of use, inability to use, or about the reliability, accuracy or sufficiency of the information contained in this book.

Made with ♥ on the Notion Press Platform
www.notionpress.com

A

Gift For

'Princess Chandrika'

On Her

13th *Birthday*

(3rd *October 2024)*

Contents

Acknowledgements

I would like to express my deepest gratitude to my wife, whose unwavering love and support have been the foundation of everything I have achieved. To my daughter, the inspiration behind this story, I hope the lessons I have learned the hard way will guide you and others like you on your journey. A heartfelt thanks to everyone around me who has shaped my worldview. I consider this book a complete reflection of your wisdom, and not mine. Thank you everyone for being part of this journey.

*   - The Author*

Legal Disclaimer

This book is a work of fiction, and any resemblance to actual persons, living or dead, or real events, is purely coincidental. The names, characters, places, and incidents portrayed are fictitious and are not intended to represent or resemble any real individuals or situations.

The concepts, values, and ideas presented in this book are meant to serve the fictional narrative and should not be taken as professional, legal, financial, or personal advice. The contents of this book are intended for entertainment purposes only, and no reader should infer any real-life application of the teachings or opinions expressed by its characters.

This book is not intended to promote or offend any family, name, surname, caste, creed, race, religion, or profession. Any references to cultural, social, or historical elements are fictionalized and not intended to convey any form of discrimination or endorsement of any such distinctions in real life.

The author and publisher disclaim any and all liability or responsibility for any actions taken by readers based on the content of this fictional work. All responsibility for personal decisions remains with the reader, and the book's contents are not meant to influence any real-life decisions or be interpreted as a source of any kind of guidance.

For all kinds of real-world advice, professional or expert consultation should always be sought.

Where Do You See Yourself 20 Years From Now?

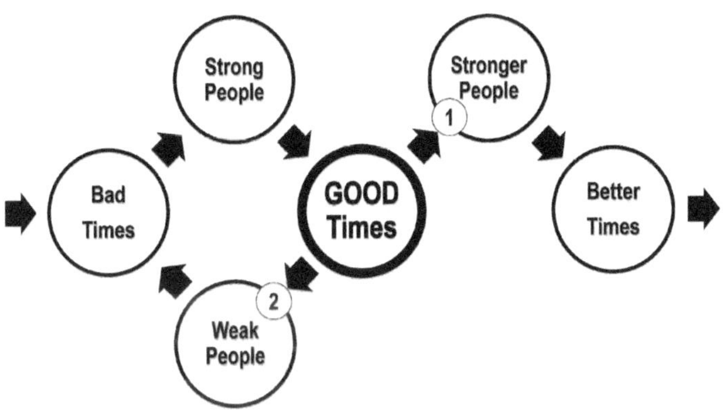

Now is your 'GOOD Times'! What will you become? Option-1 or Option-2?

Life moves in generational cycles of similar experiences, each one bringing its own rhythm of progress, growth, and reflection—unless someone stronger breaks free and takes the lead to carve a new path. Today, we find ourselves in a time of ease—"Good Times" where comfort and prosperity surround us. It is a moment to appreciate the path that has brought us here, but also a moment to pause and ask, what comes next?

Every era of ease presents a choice. As Robert Frost once wrote, "Two roads diverged in the woods," and we too must decide which path to follow. The privileges we enjoy today are the result of the hard work of those who came before us. Our world is one of greater opportunity, where education, technology, and access to resources have made life more comfortable than ever before. Yet, with this abundance comes a subtle challenge: how will we use it?

When life becomes easier, it's only natural for human beings to relax, to breathe deeply in the security of the present. This is not something to be criticized—it is simply human nature. But with comfort comes responsibility. What will we do with what we've been given? Will we use it to build a stronger foundation for the future, or will we rest on the laurels of those who paved the way?

We must recognize and honour the generations that came before us. They faced hardships, challenges, and sacrifices to build the world we enjoy today. Every privilege we have now—the ease of life, the golden spoon we've inherited—was earned through their resilience and determination. It is not enough to simply enjoy the fruits of their labour; we must continue their legacy by building upon it and making it even better.

The "golden spoon" generation, raised with access to so many luxuries, may sometimes take these privileges for granted. But this is where our deeper purpose lies. We are not just meant to enjoy the comfort—we are tasked with ensuring that we pass down something even greater to those who come after us. It is not about rejecting the comfort we've been born into, but about recognizing that it carries a responsibility to create a future that is stronger, more resilient, and deeply rooted in our own identity and family legacy.

Throughout human history, both hardship and ease have inspired growth. The road ahead is not about turning away from comfort, but about understanding that the privileges we enjoy today come with a duty to prepare for tomorrow. We are entrusted with the task of building upon what we've inherited, ensuring that it remains strong for future generations.

Today, two roads have once again diverged before us. One road invites us to continue the journey of growth, honouring the hard work of those who came before us by building on their legacy. It encourages us to use the privileges we enjoy today not merely as comforts, but as tools to strengthen our future. It is the road where we ask ourselves, "How can I contribute? How can I take what I have and improve it for those who will come after me?" This is the path that requires us to cherish our identity, preserve our family legacy, and make it even better.

The other road, while tempting in its ease, asks little of us. It invites us to simply enjoy the present, to rest on what has already been achieved without considering the future. But this road carries the risk of leaving future generations unprepared for their own challenges, potentially breaking the cycle of progress that has brought us to this moment.

The beauty of this moment lies in the possibilities it offers. Both roads are open, and the choice is ours. We are not bound by the past, nor are we victims of our circumstances. Instead, we are empowered by the privileges we have, and we hold the power to shape the future through the decisions we make today.

The abundance we enjoy now is not just a reward—it is an opportunity. It is our chance to build upon it, to create something even greater. We have the tools, the wisdom of past generations, and the responsibility to ensure that the legacy we pass down is one of strength, resilience, and beauty. It is up to us to preserve what we have, enrich it, and pass it forward.

Life's cycles will continue, as they always have. But how we choose to navigate them will determine not only our future, but the future of those who follow. Today, we are called not just to enjoy the present, but to plant the seeds for tomorrow—to preserve our family legacy and ensure that it flourishes for generations to come.

Today, we stand empowered, guided by the wisdom of the past and equipped with the resources of the present. The road ahead is full of promise, and the choices we make now will define the legacy we leave behind. You could find yourself looking back at a journey of growth, strength, and progress, having built upon the foundation given to you. Or, you might find yourself wondering what could have been if you had only taken that step forward. Will you be someone who took the easy road, or will you carve out a new path of purpose, strength, and legacy? **The decision is yours, and the future awaits. Where do you see yourself 20 years from now?**

Prologue

This fictional novel begins in the serene ambiance of Eco Park, Kolkata, where the intertwined lives of Sanjay, Sujata, and their teenage daughter Chitra unfold against the backdrop of love, ambition, and the pursuit of a meaningful life. Their journey, like the gentle ripples on the lake, touches on deep themes of growth, resilience, and legacy, woven together by their shared experiences.

Sanjay, now 45, is a man reflecting on the paths he's walked—both personal and professional. Raised in Agartala and later settling in Kolkata, his childhood was defined by traditional Bengali values of discipline, hard work, and the pursuit of stability. However, from a young age, Sanjay felt an entrepreneurial spark within him, a desire to forge his own path. His parents, government employees, encouraged a more secure career, but he managed to express his creativity in many small ways—selling sports stickers or sketching caricatures. His love for architecture led him to Maharashtra for higher studies, and from there, his career flourished. Over two decades, Sanjay built a name for himself as a successful architect and serial entrepreneur, across India and abroad. But beyond his professional accolades, his true legacy lies in the lessons he wishes to impart to Chitra.

Sanjay's journey is not just about building a career; it is about learning from the distractions, failures, and successes he encountered along the way. His story is one of resilience, moving from uncertainty to clarity, and he hopes that Chitra, now at the cusp of adolescence, will not just inherit the architectural business but the values of discipline, time management, and long-term focus that have shaped his life.

Sujata, Sanjay's wife, stands as the quiet force in their family—steady, supportive, and wise. Her own journey is marked by success and grace. Raised in Krishnagar, Sujata pursued higher education with relentless determination, completing her B.Sc. and M.Sc. from top-tier institutions before rising to the position of CEO in a prominent healthcare chain in West Bengal. Yet, despite her impressive career, Sujata never lost sight of her role as a mother and wife. Her balance between professional achievement and nurturing her family shows Chitra what it means to thrive in both spheres of life. Sujata's calm demeanour, emotional intelligence, and belief in education as a tool for growth are values she passes on to Chitra, ensuring that her daughter understands the importance of resilience and independence.

Chitra, on the brink of her teenage years, represents the future of the family. Bright and curious, she listens intently as her father begins to share his life experiences. While Sanjay is focused on ensuring that Chitra doesn't waste time on short-term distractions, Sujata encourages her to build her own identity. Chitra's character evolves through the novel as she absorbs the lessons from her parents, ready to carry forward the family's legacy—not just in the business, but in the values of perseverance, creativity, and love that bind them together.

The story explores their lives through a series of reflective conversations between Sanjay and Chitra, with Sujata often providing subtle wisdom. Sanjay speaks of his childhood in Agartala, the struggles he faced during his early years, and the lessons learned in his young adulthood when distractions and relationships pulled him away from his goals. He shares the journey of finding clarity, not just in his profession but in life, and how Sujata became his anchor through every challenge.

As the novel progresses, Chitra begins to understand the bigger picture. She sees that her parents' life lessons are not about restricting her but preparing her for a future where she can be both independent and resilient. By the end of the story, Chitra is ready to forge her own path, guided by the wisdom of her father and the quiet strength of her mother.

"Give Me Back My Time" goes beyond being just a family story—it is a meditation on the nature of time itself: how it quietly slips away, how we must be mindful in its use, and how, once spent, it is lost forever. The novel explores the delicate balance between creating a meaningful life for oneself and laying the foundation for future generations. Through the lives of Sanjay, Sujata, and Chitra, readers are invited to reflect on their own relationship with time, ambition, and the legacies they aspire to leave behind. **With themes of resilience, love, and the pursuit of dreams woven throughout, the novel illustrates how each generation builds upon the experiences of the last, creating something lasting.**

The Three Fictional Central Characters of 'Give Me Back My Time'—Sanjay, Sujata, and Chitra—play pivotal roles in shaping the narrative of the story. Through their personal growth, family dynamics, and individual values, they reflect the core themes of the book: resilience, wisdom, love, and the legacy of family.

Sanjay
The Father with a Dream…

Sanjay: The Father with a Dream

- Sanjay, at 45, is a man whose life has been shaped by resilience, hard work, and self-reflection. He is both the narrator of the story and the guide for his daughter, Chitra, as she embarks on her teenage years. Sanjay's journey is filled with life experiences that have made him the person he is today—a seasoned architect and serial entrepreneur who strives to balance the pressures of his career with his desire to be a good father and husband.
- Born and brought up in Agartala, and later settling in Kolkata, Sanjay grew up in a traditional, conservative

Bengali family, where stability and responsibility were prioritized. His parents, both government employees, moulded his early years, pushing him toward the safety of a secure job. However, Sanjay always felt a tug toward entrepreneurship, driven by the desire to create something of his own. Even as a child, his entrepreneurial spark shone through in small ways—he sold stickers of cricket players to his classmates and drew caricatures during school festivals, earning a bit of pocket money on the side.

- As Sanjay reflects on his life, he remembers the distractions and relationships that once pulled him away from his goals during his teenage years. However, through those experiences, he learned to differentiate between what truly mattered and what was fleeting. He speaks with Chitra not from a place of regret, but from the understanding that life's distractions are part of the journey toward finding clarity.
- Sanjay encourages her to stay focused on the bigger picture and to prioritize long-term goals over short-term thrills, teaching her that true success is not about avoiding distractions but learning to rise above them.
- Sanjay's role as a father goes beyond providing for his family—he wants to empower Chitra with the life experiences he's gathered. He emphasizes the importance of financial independence, time management, and the significance of relationships built on mutual growth and understanding.
- Sanjay's journey is one of self-realization and building a life of meaning, and he hopes to pass on this sense of clarity to his daughter.

Sujata

The Strong, Successful Mother...

Sujata: The Strong, Successful Mother

- Sujata is not only Sanjay's wife and Chitra's mother but also the heart of the family. Her presence is the calm that grounds both Sanjay and Chitra, and her quiet strength is what holds them together. Sujata's role in the family is one of balance—she is both a successful career woman and a nurturing mother. She grew up in Krishnagar, West Bengal, and met Sanjay when they were young. Their relationship blossomed over time, built on mutual respect and shared dreams.

- As the CEO of a prominent healthcare chain in West Bengal, Sujata is a woman who has successfully balanced her career and family life. Her rise to success in the corporate world is a testament to her hard work, intellect, and resilience. But Sujata never lets her professional achievements overshadow her family responsibilities. She understands the importance of being present for her family, particularly for Chitra, as she steps into her teenage years.

- Sujata's approach to love is pragmatic—she believes that true love is not about fleeting passion or attraction but about commitment, trust, and standing by each other through every challenge. This is the message she conveys to Chitra, showing her that love, like life, is built on the small, steady moments that create lasting bonds.

- Sujata has always supported Sanjay's entrepreneurial ambitions, knowing that their strength as a couple comes from their ability to uplift and empower each other. As she watches Sanjay pass on his wisdom to Chitra, Sujata feels a deep sense of pride in the life they've built together and the values they are imparting to their daughter.

Chitra: The Curious New Teenager

- Chitra, on the brink of adolescence, represents both the future and the continuity of the family's legacy. She has just turned 13, and with that milestone comes a growing awareness of the world around her. Chitra is curious, bright, and full of questions, eager to learn from her parents and understand the lessons they have gathered through their lives. Though she is still a child in many ways—her playful energy and wide-eyed innocence intact—there is a growing maturity in her as she begins to absorb the life experiences Sanjay shares.

- As a teenager, Chitra faces the typical distractions of her age—social media, peer pressure, and the lure of short-term gratification. Sanjay sees in her both the potential for greatness and the possibility of being led astray by these distractions. He feels it is his responsibility to guide her through this phase, teaching her the importance of focus, time management, and resilience. Chitra listens attentively to her father's stories, knowing that these lessons will shape her future.

- Chitra's role in the story is one of a learner—she is the vessel through which the wisdom of her parents' flows. However, she is not a passive recipient; Chitra is actively engaged, asking questions, reflecting on her parents' words, and beginning to form her own understanding of the world. She understands that carrying forward her family's legacy is not about blindly following in her parents' footsteps, but about building upon them with her own dreams, passions, and hard work.

- As she listens to her father talk about the importance of financial independence and time freedom, Chitra begins to realize that success is not just about working hard—it's about working smart. Sanjay's emphasis on earning money to buy back time resonates with her, as she starts to understand that true success lies in having the freedom to pursue creative and meaningful interests.

The characters of 'Give Me Back My Time'—Sanjay, Sujata, and Chitra—are deeply interconnected, each playing a vital role in the family's growth and the narrative of the novel. Sanjay, the dreamer and guide, is driven by his desire to pass on the wisdom he's gathered through life's challenges. Sujata, the anchor, provides the calm and stability that allows both Sanjay and Chitra to flourish. And Chitra, the eager learner, stands at the crossroads of childhood and adulthood, ready to inherit not just her family's legacy, but the life lessons that will guide her toward her own future. **Together, they form the heart of the story—a family bound by love, wisdom, and the shared pursuit of a meaningful life.**

1

When I Learnt Life's First Secrets

"Time is your most valuable asset, use it wisely, because once it's gone, no amount of money can bring it back."

- Sanjay

Sanjay leaned back on the bench, his gaze following the gentle ripples across the lake as the setting sun cast its warm, golden glow over Eco Park, Kolkata. The evening breeze rustled through the trees, carrying the soft laughter of families and the distant hum of the city, creating a serene atmosphere. It was a peaceful moment, perfect for reflection, with the light of the setting sun blending into soft hues of pink and orange, casting a shimmering reflection on the calm waters. The breeze cooled the air as dusk settled in, drawing the day to a close.

This was Sanjay's favourite time of day, when the noise of the world began to quiet, leaving space for contemplation. He felt the stillness of the moment, and with it, the sense that it was the right time to share something valuable with Chitra. Today was special. His daughter, Chitra, had just turned thirteen, marking a new chapter in her life. It was more than a birthday—it was the beginning of her transformation into adulthood.

The air was filled with a quiet significance, not just because of the calm evening, but because Sanjay knew that this milestone in Chitra's life was important. As the sun dipped lower, casting a soft glow on their surroundings, Sanjay realized that his role as a father had just entered a new phase. Chitra was no longer a child—she was growing into a young woman, and with that came the responsibility of guiding her through this delicate transition. Today, it wasn't just about celebrating her birthday, but also about imparting wisdom that would help shape her future.

Sitting on the wooden bench beside him, Chitra swung her legs lightly, her excitement from the day's celebration still lingering in her wide eyes. Sanjay observed her, knowing that there were things he needed to share with her. He had been waiting for the right moment, and today felt perfect. His mind drifted back to his own youth, and the life experiences he had learned—life experiences he wished he had understood sooner.

Sujata, his wife, was seated a few feet away, her attention focused on the simple task of arranging their picnic. There was something serene about the way she moved, her long hair gleaming in the last rays of sunlight as she leaned over the basket, carefully unfolding the gingham blanket. She smoothed out its edges with precision, her movements deliberate yet unhurried, reflecting her steady, calming presence in their lives. She then began arranging the food—samosas, fresh fruits, a flask of tea—each item placed thoughtfully. Her laughter, which had filled the air just moments ago, was like a melody to Sanjay's ears—unassuming, but ever-present, much like her.

Sujata had always been the foundation of their family, her calm demeanour grounding them through the whirlwind of their busy lives. Sanjay often marvelled at how effortlessly she brought order and peace to any situation, simply by being herself. Now, as he watched her, a small smile tugged at his lips. She was his anchor, the calm in his storm, and today, just as always, she held everything together while he wrestled with the weight of fatherhood.

Chitra, on the other hand, was a bundle of energy. Her wide, curious eyes sparkled with excitement from the day's celebrations. She was on the cusp of something new, stepping into the unknown world of her teenage years. Her legs swung lightly off the edge of the bench, a reminder that in some ways, she was still a child. But Sanjay could see glimmers of the young woman she would soon become. Her dark hair fell in gentle waves over her shoulders, catching the soft golden hues of the evening sun. Her smile—so much like Sujata's—lit up her face as she turned her full attention to her father.

Sanjay himself felt the weight of the moment. This was not just another day, but a milestone for Chitra, and a reflective point for him as a father. He gazed out at the sky, watching it change from orange to pink, then to soft purples as the colours blended together like watercolours on a canvas. The coolness of the bench beneath him grounded him as his thoughts travelled back to his own teenage years. He had learned so much since then—wisdom gained through joyful experiences and difficult challenges. Now, as he sat beside his daughter, he knew it was time to share those life lessons, to guide her as she stepped into the next phase of her life.

In the distance, the faint hum of traffic from the city blended with the soft rustle of the trees and the gentle chatter of passers-by. The park felt like a world apart from the bustling city life of Kolkata, a peaceful haven where time seemed to slow down just enough to allow moments like these—moments of reflection, of connection between father and daughter.

Sanjay inhaled deeply, feeling the crisp evening air fill his lungs, the scent of grass and earth mingling with the distant aroma of street food from carts near the park entrance. He felt grateful for this place, for this quiet corner of the world where they could escape the rush of daily life and simply be together. As he looked at Sujata, still diligently arranging the food, he felt a wave of gratitude wash over him. She was his partner, his anchor, and together they had built this life—a life filled with both the simple joys and the complex challenges of parenthood.

Now, as he prepared to share his life's first secrets with Chitra, he knew he wasn't just speaking as her father, but as a man who had learned, loved, and lived—much of it, thanks to the quiet strength of the woman just a few feet away. He glanced at Chitra, whose wide eyes reflected the soft glow of the evening light. "Chitra," he began, breaking the quietness of the moment, "there's something I've been wanting to talk to you about."

Chitra, still smiling from the playful teasing earlier, turned her full attention to him. Sensing that this was more than just casual conversation, she stopped swinging her legs and settled in, eager to hear what her father had to say. Her curiosity piqued. "What is it, Papa?" she asked softly.

Sanjay leaned forward, his voice softening as he began to speak about one of the most treasured moments of his life—Chitra's birth. "You know, Chitra," he started, his eyes brightening with emotion, "the day you were born was the best thing that ever happened to me."

He smiled, recalling every detail of that day. "I remember pacing back and forth outside the hospital room, my heart racing, and my mind filled with all sorts of thoughts. What kind of father would I be? How would I raise you? What would life be like with this little person who was about to enter our world?"

His voice grew quieter; the emotions clear in his tone. "And then, when I heard your first cry from outside the room, it was as if everything in the world stopped for a moment. I rushed to see you when the doctor brought you outside—almost looking like a towel wrapped strawberry ice crème! this tiny, perfect being—and I knew right then and there that my life had changed forever. The moment I saw you in the doctor's arms, suddenly all those questions I had just blurred away. Nothing else mattered but you."

He paused, letting the memories flood back. "It's funny, Chitra. I've had so many proud moments in life—my extensive career across India and abroad, building multiple businesses, so many national and international awards and achievements—but none of that compares to the joy I felt when I became your father. You were my greatest blessing, my biggest responsibility, and my deepest joy all at once."

Sanjay's smile widened as he added, "That's why, from the very beginning, I've wanted to give you the best life possible. Not in terms of things or material success, but in terms of experiences, wisdom, and love. Because that's what you deserve. You are, and always will be, the best thing that has ever happened to me."

Chitra, listening intently, could feel the depth of her father's love and the bond they shared. It was a bond that had shaped her life and would continue to guide her as she grew.

Sanjay sighed, his gaze moving toward the lake. "You're thirteen now, a big girl!" he began, "There's something I wish someone had told me when I was your age. I learned it much later in life, and by then, I had already missed many opportunities."

Chitra stopped swinging her legs, her eyes fixed on her father. She knew him as a man of few words, but when he spoke with such gravity, it always carried meaning.

Sanjay smiled faintly. "When I was your age, growing up in Agartala, everything seemed simple. It was a small, quiet town, nothing like Kolkata. We lived in an extended joint family—your grandparents, great-grandparents, my aunt, and then there was my maternal grandparent's huge family in close proximity. I was the only child for many years, and everyone doted on me. For the initial years of my childhood, I thought the world revolved only around me."

Chitra chuckled, imagining her father as a young boy, the centre of attention.

"But then," Sanjay continued, his voice softening, "things changed. My cousins were born, one after the other, and I had to learn to share—attention, affection, time. It wasn't easy for me, but it was an important life experience. The world doesn't revolve around any one person. Life moves on, with or without us at the centre. We have to learn to share space, to share love."

Chitra nodded, listening intently.

Sanjay leaned back, the nostalgia lighting up his face as he began to tell Chitra about his childhood in Agartala. "You know, Chitra," he started with a chuckle, "back in those days, there was no TV in our house, until I was almost in middle school. No phones, no internet either. We found our entertainment in the simplest things around us."

Chitra listened closely, captivated by the world her father was describing, a world so different from her own.

"Your grandfather had a transferable job and he had to keep travelling, and because of my schooling, me and your grandmother could not always travel with him. So, I was often for weeks or even months together, at my maternal grandparent's home in a beautiful small village beside the picturesque Durga Bari Tea Estate near Agartala, where everything moved at a slower pace, and honestly, we didn't mind. We'd wake up early to the sound of birds, not alarms. The day started with a cup of tea for the elders, and for us kids, it meant running out barefoot into the open, playing with whatever we could find—a stick, an old ball, or even dried leaves or just mud. If you could imagine it, we could play it. I even remember trying to make miniature buildings with clay and broken bricks and sticks and other stuff, trying to mimic the masons who were constructing our house. As I reflect now it seems that my natural inclination towards architecture was very early on."

Sanjay smiled wider. "The best part was how the whole neighbourhood felt like family. If you weren't at your own house, someone knew exactly where to find you. We were always at someone's doorstep, sharing snacks or stories. In the afternoons, after lunch, all the kids would gather under some tree near the village temple. We played marbles, gilli-danda, kabaddi, hide-and-seek, and what not until dusk. The more dust-covered we were, the better the day had been!"

Chitra's eyes were wide, absorbing every detail. "No playgrounds?" she asked, amazed.

Sanjay laughed. "Who needed playgrounds when we had nature? The open fields were our playgrounds. We climbed trees like monkeys, ran around the dry paddy fields, climbed up the sloped roof tops or up some nearby hillocks, and during the rainy season, we'd race paper boats in the puddles. The rain? Oh, it wasn't a nuisance. It was a reason to run outside and get soaked while elders yelled at us from the porch!"

He paused, letting the memory settle before continuing. "We used to make our own toys—kite-flying competitions would last for days, and if you cut someone's kite, oh, it was a moment of glory! And during festivals like Durga Puja, we'd go for pandal hopping, visit house to house, collecting gifts and sweets, it was a completely free life, just joyful."

Chitra smiled at the thought of her father as a boy, running through fields, creating his own adventures. It was a simpler time, one that had shaped him into the resilient and creative man she knew today.

Sanjay had been narrating stories from his childhood to Chitra for a while now, each memory seemed to bring him back to a simpler time in Agartala. Chitra, sitting beside him, listened intently, hanging on to every word. There was something magical in the way her father brought those stories to life.

"And then," Sanjay continued, his voice soft with nostalgia, "there was this door-to-door bear dance."

Chitra looked up, curious. "Bear dance?"

Sanjay smiled, the image vivid in his mind. "Yes, when I was very young, it wasn't monkeys that would come dancing door to door. It was bears! A man would walk through the neighbourhood, leading a big brown bear on a rope, making it dance to the beat of a small drum. It was a huge thing for us kids, watching something so wild and majestic right there in front of our homes."

Chitra's eyes widened with disbelief. "A bear? Really, Papa?"

He chuckled. "Oh yes, a real bear. I remember the excitement we all felt. The moment we heard the drum, we'd run out to see it. The bear would stand on its hind legs, swaying and moving to the rhythm, as if it knew the tune. It felt like the most incredible thing back then."

Chitra giggled, thinking back to her recent experience. "That sounds a lot like the monkey dance I saw a few years back! You know, the one that came in front of our house right?"

Sanjay nodded, his smile fading just slightly as he looked at her. "Exactly. But you see, Chitra, just like with that monkey, what seemed so entertaining to us as kids wasn't so good for the animals themselves. Back then, we didn't realize the bear was only performing because it was trained through cruel means. The poor thing was made to dance not because it wanted to, but because it had no choice."

Chitra's face grew thoughtful as she compared her recent encounter with the monkey. "So, it wasn't as fun for the animals as it seemed to us?"

Sanjay shook his head. "No, it wasn't. We were just kids, so we didn't think about it. We were mesmerized by the show, just like you were with the monkey! But now, looking back, I understand that while we were entertained, the animals were suffering. They were taken from their natural habitat, forced to perform, and that's no life for them."

Chitra looked down, reflecting on the lesson her father had just imparted. "I never thought about it like that."

Sanjay gave her a reassuring smile. "That's the thing, Chitra. Sometimes, the things that seem fun or innocent at first have a much bigger story behind them. It's important to look beyond what's right in front of us and think about how others—whether they're people or animals—are affected."

Chitra nodded, her gaze shifting to the lake nearby as she quietly absorbed the lesson. The stories her father told, filled with light-hearted moments, always seemed to have a deeper meaning. Today's conversation was no different, as it gently steered her from amusement to empathy and understanding.

Chitra, still deep in thought from her father's story, suddenly perked up. Without saying a word, she got up from the bench and ran over to her mother, who was busy setting up the picnic on the grass nearby. "Can I have a cookie, Ma?" she asked, her eyes lighting up as Sujata handed her a small, round treat. Chitra smiled, clutching her prize, and hurried back to sit beside Sanjay. She leaned into her father as she nibbled on the cookie, ready for the next part of his story.

Sanjay watched her with affection, his heart full as he prepared to continue the journey through his childhood, this time about the grandparents who had played such a pivotal role in his life. His thoughts travelled back to his childhood. His parents, both government employees, had lived their lives seeking stability. "You know Chitra," he said, "your grandparents believed that life was all about finding security—a steady job, a predictable income. They wanted that for me too. In their eyes, it was the safest way to live."

Chitra had heard about her grandparents before, but today, her father's tone was different—more personal, more reflective.

"They are good people," Sanjay continued, "but they saw the world in a particular way. They thought life was about stability and safety. But I... I wasn't like them. Even when I was your age, I felt this pull—this desire to do something more. I didn't know what it was, but I knew I wanted to create something, to build something of my own."

Chitra leaned in, intrigued by this glimpse into her father's younger self.

"When I was around your age," Sanjay smiled, "I started creating stickers of famous cricketers. I spent hours making sure every detail was perfect. Then I'd try to sell them to my classmates for a few rupees. It wasn't much, but it gave me a taste of something I hadn't felt before—freedom. I had created something with my own hands, and I earned money from it. It was exhilarating."

Chitra's eyes lit up. "You sold stickers?" she asked, surprised.

Sanjay nodded, chuckling softly. "Yes, I did. It seems small now, but back then, it felt like the world to me."

"But my grandparents didn't see it that way, did they?" Chitra guessed.

Sanjay shook his head. "No, to them, it was a distraction. They thought it was a waste of time—something that pulled me away from my studies. They didn't understand why I was so interested in something so... unimportant."

He paused, his gaze fixed on the horizon, as if he could see his younger self reflected in the ripples of the lake. "And that's when I learned Chitra, that not everyone will understand your dreams. Not everyone will see the things that are important to you in the same way you do. But that doesn't mean you should stop pursuing them."

Chitra sat quietly, absorbing her father's words. The life experience was taking root in her mind.

The afternoon sun was sinking slowly, casting long shadows across Eco Park as the golden light bathed everything in a warm glow. The air was still comfortable, holding on to the last remnants of the day's heat, but there was a hint of the evening coolness yet to come. The trees swayed gently, their leaves rustling softly in the breeze that carried the subtle scent of grass and nearby flowers. Ducks could be seen lazily swimming in the lake, their ripples shimmering in the dappled sunlight. In the distance, the muffled sounds of laughter and chatter from families enjoying their afternoon lingered in the background, blending into the calm and peaceful surroundings.

"You see," Sanjay continued, "growing up, I didn't have many friends by the time I was of your age. Your grandparents were strict, and they wanted me to focus on my studies. So, I spent a lot of time alone—with my books, with my crafts, with my thoughts. It was alone at times, but not lonely for sure, because I was happy with myself. And in those solitary days, I learned something valuable."

He looked at Chitra, his expression serious but kind. "I learned that sometimes, being alone helps you discover who you really are. It gives you space to think, to dream, to figure out what you want in life. That's something you should remember as you grow older."

Chitra nodded, her eyes wide and thoughtful.

"But there's more," Sanjay said, his voice soft but firm. "It's not just about knowing what you want. It's about acting consciously—not out of habit, not because of what others expect, but because you've thought it through. Every decision you make should come from that place of conscious thought, not compulsion."

He paused, watching Chitra carefully. "That means you need to make deliberate choices—whether it's about your friends, your life partner, your career, your health, your wealth, or as simple as how you spend your own time. Don't just react to life—respond to it. Take control of it."

Chitra absorbed her father's advice. The weight of his words settled deeply within her.

"And one more thing, Chitra," Sanjay added, his tone softening once again. "Financial independence. It's something I didn't understand until much later in life, but it's so important. When you have your own money, you have choices. You're not dependent on anyone else. And I want you to have that freedom. That's why I've built this business—not just for me, but for you."

Chitra looked up at him, understanding dawning on her face.

"Life isn't just about working for someone else," Sanjay continued, his voice carrying the life experiences from his own hard-earned experiences. "It's also about creating something for yourself—multiple streams of income that give you the freedom to make your own decisions. You're not trapped just by one job, one paycheck. Taking up a job as a career maybe one of the many sources of your revenue, but should not be the only one. Diversify your portfolio. Be in control."

The evening light had almost faded, the stars beginning to twinkle above them. The world felt quiet and still, as if the park itself was listening to Sanjay's words.

"I understand, Papa," Chitra said softly. "I'll remember."

Sanjay smiled, feeling a deep sense of peace. He stood, offering his hand to Chitra, and together they walked over to join Sujata on the mat. As they sat down for their picnic, the night sky above them, Sanjay felt gratitude for the opportunity to pass on these life experiences—life experiences that would guide Chitra as she stepped into her future.

As they observed other people at a distance, lazily strolling down the tree-lined path, with the twinkling starts coming up gently overhead, Sanjay's thoughts shifted. He glanced at Chitra, her movements light but her gaze thoughtful, as if she were reflecting on everything they had just spoken. There were some more crucial life experiences he wanted to impart, something that had shaped his own path but he knew was often overlooked by many.

"Chitra," he began, his tone more serious but still warm, "I want you to remember something as you grow older. You are the average of five friends around you!"

Sujata's lips curved into a gentle smile, a quiet expression of warmth and understanding that softened her entire face.

Chitra looked at him, slightly puzzled. "What do you mean, Papa?"

Sanjay smiled. "It's simple. The people you surround yourself with have a huge influence on who you become. If you're around people who are driven, positive, motivated, entrepreneurial, and always striving to improve themselves, you'll naturally adopt those qualities too. But if you're around people who settle for mediocrity or don't push themselves to grow, you'll find yourself slowly becoming like them too, even if you don't mean to."

Chitra furrowed her brow, absorbing this new idea. "So, it's important to choose my friends carefully?"

"Exactly," Sanjay said, his voice softening. "The friends you keep will shape how you think, how you feel, how you behave, how you score in the exams, and even how much you earn! It's not just about avoiding bad influences—it's about actively surrounding yourself with people who inspire you to be better. People who challenge you to grow, to learn, and to aim higher."

He paused, watching her closely. "Think of it this way: if you want to be successful, if you want to live a life that's meaningful, you have to be with people who are also pursuing their best selves. You will always rise to the level of the people you spend the most time with. That's why you need to choose your circle carefully."

Chitra nodded slowly, the weight of his words sinking in. It was yet another subtle life life experience she realized not everyone was taught at her age, but one that could make all the difference in the long run.

Sanjay gave her a reassuring smile. "It's a life experience that not all of your friends will hear from their parents, but trust me—it's one of the most important ones."

In the stillness of that evening, surrounded by the warmth of his family, Sanjay knew that Chitra's journey had just begun—but she was armed with the knowledge he wished he had received earlier. And that, he hoped, would make all the difference.

As they sat under the twilight sky, with stars beginning to twinkle here and there, the quiet hum of the park around them, Sanjay turned to Chitra with a softness in his voice. The breeze, cool and calming, gently rustled the leaves, carrying with it a sense of peaceful introspection. Chitra sat beside her father, her eyes reflecting the twinkling sky above, waiting for his next words, sensing that this conversation would carry weight.

"Chitra," Sanjay began, his voice deliberate and thoughtful, "you are growing up in a world where it's easy to look around and feel like you need to be like everyone else. I see how your friends live their lives, how they chase trends and follow each other, and I know how tempting it can be to want to fit in. But, I need you to understand something—don't ever try to be like someone else."

Chitra looked at her father, puzzled. "But Papa, isn't it good to learn from others, to see how they live, and follow what works for them?"

Sanjay smiled, the lines around his eyes softening. "Of course, beta, we should always learn from others. Life is full of life experiences that can come from the most unexpected places. But learning doesn't mean imitation. You can observe someone's journey, take note of their struggles and victories, but trying to live their life, follow their path exactly—it will only make you lose sight of who you are. You see, everyone's journey is different. Their parents, their family, their upbringing, their dreams, their strengths, their challenges are not yours."

Chitra nodded, though she was still trying to grasp what her father was getting at. Sanjay noticed her hesitation and continued, his tone even more gentle now. "Think about it this way," he said, pointing to the lake in front of them. "Each wave in this lake is different. Some are small, some are big, but they all move at their own pace. If one wave tried to move like the other, it would lose its rhythm, its flow. You are your own wave, Chitra. You have your own rhythm."

Chitra's eyes widened slightly as she began to see the analogy her father was painting. "But, Papa, sometimes it's hard. It feels like everyone else has their life figured out. They all seem to know what they're doing, and I feel like I'm just... lost."

Sanjay's gaze softened as he placed a hand on her shoulder. "I understand, beta. It's natural to feel that way sometimes. But trust me, no one has it all figured out. Everyone is struggling with something, even if they don't show it. And the more you try to be like them, the more lost you will feel. Life isn't about fitting into someone else's shoes. It's about finding your own space, your own purpose."

He paused for a moment, letting his words settle in the evening air. "Take me, for example," he continued. "I learned from my teachers, my mentors, and even my colleagues. But I never tried to be like them. I took what I needed, adapted it to my own life, found my own way, and moved on in life. That's what I want for you. Learn from others, yes, but always, always stay true to yourself."

Chitra leaned her head against her father's arm, a silent acknowledgment of the wisdom he was passing on. "So, you're saying I should create my own life, not try to live like someone else?"

Sanjay smiled. "Exactly. It's good to admire people, to be inspired by them, but don't forget—you have your own journey, your own story to write. Don't let anyone else's life dictate yours."

Chitra thought about her friends, how often she compared herself to them, and how she sometimes felt like she wasn't enough. But sitting here now, under the stars with her father, she realized that maybe she didn't need to keep up with anyone else. Maybe her path was hers to discover, in her own time.

"You're right, Papa," she said quietly. "I'll try to remember that."

Sanjay squeezed her shoulder gently. "Good. You don't need to be anyone else, Chitra. You are enough, just as you are. And the world needs you, not a copy of someone else."

The two sat in comfortable silence for a while, the evening embracing them in its quiet warmth. Chitra felt a sense of relief wash over her, knowing that she didn't have to rush, didn't have to be like everyone else. She could take her time, learn, earn, grow, and most importantly, be herself.

Sanjay gazed at his daughter, pride swelling in his heart. He knew she would face many challenges, many pressures to conform, but he also knew that she had the strength to stay true to who she was. And that, he thought, was more important than anything else.

Sanjay chuckled softly, remembering something, shook his head. "You know, it's a shame that most people still think there's something as a stable job, beta. I have seen people, including myself, chase after 'stable' jobs thinking it will give lifelong security, but it was really like chasing after the biggest myth. Thinking a job is safe because we've got a fat paycheck coming in every month? Trust me, nothing in life is stable anymore, especially not a job. In today's world, the moment you stop learning or the company has squeezed the last drop of life-juice out of you, you'll either be replaced, or you'll resign out of sheer frustration. The days of lifelong jobs are over."

Chitra wanted to know more. The sinking sun's soft rays reflected in her curious eyes as she turned to Sanjay. "So, you're saying I shouldn't be looking for a stable job at all?"

Sanjay shook his head again, this time with a broader smile. "Having a job is fine, but it shouldn't be your only income source. And it shouldn't eat up all you time and energy either. You can work somewhere to learn some specialized skills, but you have to keep building on the side—whether it is taking care of our own family business, or your own investments, a side hustle, or any freelance work. That way, if your job disappears tomorrow, you won't be left scrambling. People are so busy trying to 'secure' their future that they don't realize they're boxing themselves into a corner. It's a myth to think that sticking to one thing will keep you safe. Life doesn't work that way anymore. You need to be adaptable, have your hands in a few things at once. What you need to do is embrace flexibility. The 'Gig Economy' is the future. Look around—there are freelancers, consultants, small business owners, all of them making their own way. Instead of putting all your eggs in one basket, you've got to diversify. Have multiple sources of income. If one dries up, you've got another. Stay flexible, invest in learning new skills, and most importantly—don't depend on any one thing for your livelihood. It's all about creating a diversified portfolio of income streams."

Chitra laughed, feeling a sense of freedom in the idea. "Well, Papa, looks like the new normal isn't about playing it safe. It's about playing it smart."

Sanjay laughed aloud, his heart filled with joy. His daughter, at such a young age, was already grasping what had taken him years to fully understand. He patted her shoulder, proud of how quickly she was catching on to the life experiences he had spent years navigating himself.

They got up and began strolling through the park. As they walked, the evening breeze gently caressing their faces, Sanjay sensed it was time to share another life experience with Chitra. It wasn't the kind of life experience found in books, but one forged through the fires of experience, a truth that had taken him almost half of his lifetime to fully comprehend.

"Chitra," he began softly, breaking the silence, "there's something I've been meaning to talk to you about. It's a life experience that might seem simple but can make all the difference in how you live your life. Do you know what that is?"

Chitra glanced up at him, curious. "What, Papa?"

"Never foul-mouth anyone, Chitra," Sanjay said, his voice gentle but firm. "Not even behind their back. It might seem harmless, maybe even satisfying in the moment, but in the long run, it only harms you. It builds up a kind of bitterness inside, a grumpiness that eats away at your peace. You see, when you let your frustration or anger spill out in the form of harsh words about others, it's like carrying poison in your heart."

Chitra listened, her eyes wide, soaking in the gravity of her father's words.

Sanjay smiled, sensing her attentiveness. "When we speak ill of someone, be it in school, in college, in office, in family, or anywhere, we might think we're getting even, taking revenge, or venting, but what we're really doing is weighing ourselves down. And let me tell you this—most of the time, those people don't even know, nor do they care. So why should you let them have power over your peace? Why should their behaviour dictate how happy or content you feel?"

Chitra looked thoughtful, processing what her father was saying. "But Papa," she asked quietly, "what if someone really hurts you? Isn't it natural to feel upset?"

Sanjay nodded, his face soft with understanding. "Of course, it's natural to feel hurt. We're all human, and we feel things deeply. But here's the secret, beta: You can't control how others behave, but you can always control how you respond. Your ears are your own so keep them closed, and your mouth is your own so keep it shut. You can decide whether you let their actions ruin your peace or whether you rise above it. Why let their negativity take hold of your happiness?"

He paused, letting the words sink in. "Think of it like this: Life is full of all kinds of people. Some will be kind, some will be indifferent, and some will hurt you. But that's just life, Chitra. It's not about expecting everyone to be nice or everything to go your way. It's about learning not to let other people's behaviour dictate your state of mind. Don't let anyone rob you of your happiness, your peace."

Chitra furrowed her brow slightly. "So, you're saying we should just... let things go?"

Sanjay smiled at her, a warm, fatherly smile. "Not exactly. It's not about letting things go all the time. If something is truly wrong, stand up for yourself. Speak out if you must, but do it without malice. Do it without letting bitterness settle in your heart. I know it is easier said than done, and it will take some time and experience to master this, but understand this that the more grumpy, judgmental, or angry you become, the more it clouds your own mind. And that does nothing to those who've hurt you—it only damages you, and you alone."

He stopped for a moment, turning to face her fully. "Remember this, Chitra: No matter what happens around you, you can always choose how you feel. You can decide to be at peace, to be happy, regardless of others. That's the one thing no one can take from you—your ability to decide how you feel. So don't let the world steal that from you."

Chitra looked up at him, her eyes bright with newfound understanding. "You mean... I can choose to be happy, no matter what anyone else says or does?"

Sanjay nodded, his heart swelling with pride. "Exactly. That's the real power you hold, Chitra. You can't control the world, but you can control how you respond to it. And the sooner you realize that, the freer you'll be. Because you are a 'Balwaan'!"

Chitra laughed at the joke, her light giggles filling the quietness of the evening, easing the reflective mood between them.

The evening sky stretched endlessly above them, the stars shimmering like distant promises of peace. And as they walked side by side, Chitra felt something shift within her—a quiet determination to hold on to her peace, to not let the world dictate her happiness.

Sanjay smiled to himself, knowing that his daughter was growing into someone who would rise above the noise of life, holding her happiness close, no matter what life threw her way.

"Chitra," he said softly, "life moves in cycles, each generation experiencing its own moments of growth, progress, and reflection. But the truth is, unless someone stronger steps up and carves a new path, these cycles repeat. Today, we find ourselves in what many would call 'Good Times.' We're surrounded by comfort and opportunity, enjoying the fruits of hard work and sacrifice from the generations before us. And it's important to pause and appreciate that. But I want you to ask yourself, what comes next?"

Chitra nodded, listening intently as Sanjay continued.

"You see, every era of ease presents us with a choice. Robert Frost once wrote, 'Two roads diverged in the woods,' and we too must decide which path we will take. The privileges you enjoy today—the education, the technology, the comforts—are the result of the hard work of those who came before you. These things didn't just appear; they were built. And now, with all this abundance, we face a subtle challenge. How will we use it?

"When life is easy, it's natural for us to relax, to breathe deeply and enjoy the security we have. There's no shame in that—it's part of being human. But comfort also brings responsibility. We have to ask ourselves, 'What will we do with what we've been given?' Will we use it to build a stronger future, or will we rest on the efforts of the past?"

Sanjay's voice softened as he spoke about the generations that had come before them. "We must honour those who paved the way. Your grandparents, their parents, and their parents, all the way back—each generation faced hardships and challenges to build the world you live in now. Every privilege you have, Chitra, is because of their resilience and determination. But it's not enough just to enjoy what they've built. We have a responsibility to take that legacy and make it even better."

Chitra's eyes met her father's, and Sanjay could see that she understood. He smiled and continued, "You are part of what people might call the 'golden spoon' generation. Raised with so much already at your fingertips, it's easy to take these things for granted. But this is where your deeper purpose lies. You aren't meant to just enjoy the comfort you've inherited. Your task is to ensure you leave behind something greater for those who come after you. It's not about rejecting the comfort, but about recognizing the responsibility that comes with it."

He paused for a moment, allowing the weight of his words to settle in. "Throughout human history, both hardship and ease have inspired growth. The road ahead isn't about turning away from comfort. It's about understanding that with the privileges we enjoy today, there is a duty to prepare for tomorrow. We are entrusted with building on what we've inherited so it remains strong for future generations."

Sanjay pointed toward the horizon, as if indicating the roads Frost had written about. "Today, two roads have once again diverged before us. One road leads to continued growth, a path of strength where we honour the past by building on its legacy. It's where we ask, 'How can I take what I've been given and make it better for those who come after me?' This is the path where we preserve our identity, hold on to our family legacy, and strengthen it."

"And the other road," he said thoughtfully, "while easy, asks little of us. It lets us simply enjoy the present without considering the future, like many of your peers would chose to do. But that road carries the risk of leaving future generations unprepared for their challenges."

Sanjay leaned closer to Chitra. "The beauty of this moment is the possibility it offers. Both roads are open, and the choice is yours. You're not bound by the past, nor are you a victim of your circumstances. You have the power to shape the future, guided by the privileges you've inherited. The abundance you enjoy now is an opportunity, not just a reward. You can use it to create something even greater than what you were born into."

"Remember, Chitra," Sanjay concluded, his voice filled with warmth, "life's cycles will always continue. How we choose to navigate them will determine our future—and the future of those who follow. Today, you're not just called to enjoy the present, but to plant seeds for tomorrow. To make sure our family legacy thrives for generations to come."

He smiled at her gently, his eyes shining with hope. **"The road ahead is full of promise, and the choices you make now will define the legacy you leave behind. Which path will you choose today?"**

ᐛᐛᐛ

My Top 10 Learnings:

1. **The Importance of Reflection:** Sanjay emphasizes the value of reflecting on life's milestones, using moments of peace and stillness to assess progress and purpose.
2. **Cherishing Life's Milestones:** Sanjay shares how the birth of his daughter, Chitra, was the most significant moment of his life, surpassing all his professional achievements.
3. **Life's Simplest Joys:** Growing up in a small town, Sanjay learned that happiness and entertainment do not come from material wealth but from appreciating the simplicity of nature and relationships.
4. **Lessons in Sharing and Adaptability:** Sanjay learned at an early age the importance of sharing attention and love when his cousins were born, teaching him that the world does not revolve around any one person.
5. **Time Over Money:** One of Sanjay's key lessons is that time is more valuable than money because it cannot be regained. He urges Chitra to be wise with how she uses her time, focusing on meaningful and purposeful activities.
6. **Financial Independence:** Sanjay highlights the significance of financial independence, especially for young women. He teaches Chitra to rely on multiple streams of income to ensure financial security.
7. **Building on What You Have:** Rather than only enjoying what you inherit, Sanjay encourages Chitra to build upon her family's legacy, adding her own strengths and dreams to it.
8. **The Danger of Complacency:** Sanjay warns that resting on one's laurels, especially in times of comfort, can be detrimental. Instead, he emphasizes the importance of continuing to grow and challenge oneself.

9. **Long-term Thinking:** Sanjay advises Chitra to choose her career and life path based on sustainability and long-term fulfilment, not just on passion or fleeting interest.

10. **The Value of Education and Knowledge:** Learning is a continuous journey. Sanjay emphasizes that the more one learns, the more they can achieve and help others, leading to greater personal fulfilment and happiness.

2

When I Moved On From Distractions To Clarity

"*What seems very important as a teenager may not at all be relevant later, so focus on your goals, and don't let any short-term thrills pull you away from the bigger picture of your future.*"

- Sujata

Sujata sat a few feet away, quietly absorbed in her task, her hands moving with a deliberate grace as she set out the picnic. The soft evening light played across her face, casting a warm glow that made her appear almost serene, as if the world around her held no weight. Sanjay watched her for a moment, feeling the familiar pull of gratitude and affection. There was something unspoken between them, a quiet understanding built over the years. Sujata, with her calm presence, had always been the steadying force in his life. Her silent strength was what allowed him to navigate the uncertainties of fatherhood, knowing that she was there, always anchoring them to the present, no matter what.

The gentle breeze from the lake in Eco Park had begun to grow cooler, wrapping around Sanjay and Chitra as they walked up to a wooden bench and sat. The rustling leaves above them added a soft soundtrack to the moment, grounding the air with an almost meditative calm.

The light was fading quickly now, the pinks and oranges of the sky giving way to deep purples. Even more stars were beginning to appear, scattered like tiny diamonds in the darkening sky. The quiet of the evening settled around them, and Sanjay knew it was the perfect moment to continue his story—one filled with life experiences that he hoped would guide Chitra as she stepped into adulthood.

After their earlier conversation, where Sanjay had shared the first few life experiences of his life, there was still more to say. He had spoken of his childhood in Agartala, growing up around a large joint family, and the early life experiences he learned about sharing and accepting change. But now, it was time to speak of his own teen years—one filled with distractions, relationships, and the life experiences that came from navigating them.

Chitra sat beside him, her eyes wide with curiosity, waiting for her father to speak again. Sanjay could see in her the same eagerness he once felt, and he knew that what he was about to share would resonate with her now that she was a teenager herself.

"Chitra," Sanjay began, his voice softened by the weight of reflection, "you know, the choices I made as I got older shaped me just as much as my childhood did. By the time I was in my late teens, I thought I had life all figured out. But, as life does, it had other plans."

Chitra watched him closely, sensing that her father was about to share something more personal than usual.

"It was when I left Agartala," Sanjay continued, his mind drifting to those early years. "I was nineteen, heading off to Maharashtra to start my architecture studies. I was full of excitement, a little nervous too. It felt like the beginning of something big. But, with freedom, as you'll learn, comes a few distractions—many I hadn't anticipated."

Chitra tilted her head, intrigued. "Distractions, Papa?"

Sanjay smiled faintly, remembering. "The kind that can sneak up on you if you're not careful. There I was, no parents around to check on me, feeling like I had all the freedom in the world. I thought I could handle it all." He paused, his smile growing. "But that's when life throws curveballs."

Before he could continue, Sujata, who had been quietly listening, couldn't contain her laughter any longer. "Distractions? Few distractions? Oh, Chitra, did you know your father had quite a line of Girlfriends back then?" Her voice was playful, full of teasing energy.

Chitra's eyes widened in mock disbelief. "Papa? Really? A line of Girlfriends?"

Sanjay cleared his throat, now on the defensive. "Now, now, let's not get carried away," he said, throwing a quick glance at Sujata. "It wasn't exactly a line. I was always more of a one-at-a-time kind of guy."

Sujata, clearly enjoying his discomfort, shook her head with a grin. "Oh, come on, don't be shy. Chitra deserves to know her father's 'illustrious' past."

Chitra giggled, leaning in. "Tell me more, Mamma! What did Papa do? Was he some kind of romantic hero?"

Sanjay raised his hands in mock surrender, chuckling. "Alright, alright. There were a few distractions, yes. But none of them were serious. Well... maybe one."

Sujata couldn't resist adding with a smirk, "Oh yes, the 'one' who didn't even make it past your final semester exams?"

Chitra, now fully enjoying the banter, laughed. "So, what happened, Papa?"

Sanjay smiled, looking out at the lake. "Well, there was one of them who stood out. At the time, I thought she was the one. But what I didn't realize was how much of my focus had shifted. I was pouring so much time and energy into trying to manage a failing relationship that I lost sight of my studies and my dreams."

Chitra's eyebrows shot up. "You got distracted by love?"

Sanjay chuckled softly. "It wasn't love, Chitra. Back then, I confused passion and attraction with love, but real love is so much more than that. It's about commitment, about choosing to stay even when things aren't easy. Love is resilience, the ability to hold on and support each other when everything seems to be falling apart. It's the unwavering faith you have in your partner, knowing you'll face life's ups and downs together. I didn't understand that until I was with your mother. Before that, I thought I knew it all. I believed I had everything under control, but without even realizing it, I started losing sight of what truly mattered."

Sujata chimed in again, this time with a gentler smile. "That's the thing, beta. Growing up is about making those mistakes and learning from them."

Sanjay nodded, his expression turning thoughtful. "You see, relationships aren't just about emotions. They're about understanding and communication, and back then, I didn't fully get that. Men and women often express their needs differently. Men are like rubber bands—when we feel overwhelmed or need to process things, we tend to pull away, seeking a bit of distance. It's not that we don't care, it's just how we recharge. Once we've had that space, we naturally bounce back and reconnect, just like a rubber band snapping back into place. Women, on the other hand, are more like waves. Your emotions rise and fall. When you feel supported, you're on top of the wave, but when stress or emotions build up, you may feel like you're crashing. But don't worry—just like waves, you always rise again. Understanding these differences is key in relationships, as it helps us support each other better."

Chitra nodded, her face serious now, absorbing her father's words.

"The most important lesson I learned," Sanjay continued, "was that you have to communicate clearly in any relationship. If you don't, misunderstandings will happen. And that's what led to everything going off track."

Sujata smiled softly now, nodding in agreement. "We all learn that eventually."

Sanjay turned to Chitra, his voice gentler. "And when I met your mother, I finally understood what real partnership meant—someone who supports you, who helps you grow rather than hold you back. It's not about the distractions or mistakes, it's about the growth that comes after."

Chitra grinned. "So Mama, you weren't a distraction?"

Sujata, sitting nearby, winked mischievously and laughed. "No, I kept him focused!"

Sanjay laughed too. "She's right. We learned together, and that's what matters most in any relationship—growing, together. That's the key."

Chitra laughed along with her parents' playful teasing, but as the conversation settled, the mood in the air shifted subtly. The laughter faded, and a quiet, reflective silence filled the space. Chitra, still smiling from the light-hearted banter, began to feel the deeper meaning behind her father's words. What had started as a humorous recount of youthful distractions had evolved into something more significant.

As the echoes of the laughter faded, Chitra realized that her father wasn't just telling stories; he was sharing life lessons. There was more to these stories than the fun of looking back—they held meaning about choices, balance, and what it truly means to build something lasting.

She sat quietly, processing the deeper message beneath the humour. The stories about distractions and relationships weren't just amusing anecdotes from her father's past—they were lessons. Sanjay's words about love, commitment, and focus echoed in her mind, and suddenly, what had seemed like light-hearted teasing carried much more meaning.

As she glanced between her parents, she saw something new—an understanding of the depth and effort that went into their relationship. Her father's reflections on losing balance, his realization that love was more than passion, and his mother's quiet strength all came together in her mind.

Chitra watched her mother sitting calmly on the grass, smiling softly as she arranged the picnic. The way her parents spoke to each other, the way they supported one another—it felt like more than just love. It was something built with patience and care, a bond that had weathered time. Chitra found herself thinking deeply about what her father had said. His story wasn't just about the past; it was a lesson for the future—for her future.

Could she one-day experience that kind of partnership? Something rooted in trust, communication, and resilience? It was a lot to take in, but as she observed the quiet connection between her parents, she realized how much she had yet to learn about love and life.

Sanjay smiled, glancing at Chitra as he reflected on the deeper meaning of love and the invaluable lessons he had learned over the years. He had spoken about commitment, faith, and resilience, and now his thoughts naturally turned toward the one person who had taught him the true essence of those values. His words trailed off, and he let out a soft sigh, as if acknowledging an unspoken truth.

He turned his gaze toward Sujata, who sat on the grass, arranging their picnic spread with her usual calm precision. She looked up briefly, her serene smile sending him that familiar wave of comfort—a reminder of the steady anchor she had always been. That simple smile, warm and quiet, grounded him in a way nothing else ever could, assuring him that no matter how heavy the burdens might get, they would always carry them together. Her presence in his life was like the quiet flow of a river, shaping everything gently but steadily around it without making a sound. He often wondered how he had been fortunate enough to have her by his side through every high and low.

The past 17 years of their married life had been a journey filled with shared dreams, challenges, and unspoken understandings. Through every up and down, they had built a life together, piece by piece, creating a bond that felt almost unshakable. In moments of joy, they celebrated quietly, and in times of hardship, they leaned on each other without question. It was this quiet resilience that defined their relationship—one built on trust, mutual respect, and the simple, yet profound, act of always being there for one another.

Sanjay continued, his voice filled with love and warmth, "Your mother and I, we had to learn how to handle conflict, how to express love in ways that the other could understand. She expresses love through actions—through taking care of things, being there for me when I need her. I express it through words. We had to figure out how to balance those differences."

Chitra looked at her parents, trying to imagine how they navigated their relationship with so much understanding.

Sanjay continued, his tone thoughtful. "And another thing I want you to remember, Chitra—don't try to change people. That was a mistake I had made in my life. I thought that if I worked hard enough, I could change someone else to fit into what I needed. But that's not how it works. You can't mould someone into what you want them to be. You have to accept them as they are, or any relationship won't last."

Chitra nodded, listening carefully.

"One of the most important things I learned from my time with your mother is that men and women handle stress differently," Sanjay said, his voice softer now. "When I'm stressed, I withdraw. I need space to think, to figure things out. But your mother—she wants to talk through things when she's stressed. It's something we've had to navigate carefully over the years, and it's a life experience I want you to carry with you."

He turned to Chitra, his expression serious but warm. "Remember, Chitra, that in any relationship, there will be times when you and your partner approach things differently. Men often withdraw, while women seek closeness. It's not about one way being better than the other—it's about understanding those differences and navigating them with care."

Sujata couldn't hold back her laughter as she sat on the picnic mat, carefully arranging the food, looked up at Sanjay with a playful smirk. "So, all these life lessons—years of wisdom, huh? Not from someone you met in school, I hope?" she teased lightly, her tone dripping with mock suspicion.

Sanjay chuckled, shaking his head. "No, no, no credit to anyone from back then. Everything I've learned comes from living—really living—and especially over the last 17 years with you." His smile was warm, and his eyes held a sincerity that made Sujata roll her eyes affectionately. "Honestly, it's the life experiences we've shared together—figuring things out, facing challenges, building this life—that have taught me more than anything else."

Sujata leaned back on the mat, still grinning. "Well, as long as you remember that."

Chitra, watching her parents' exchange with amusement, chimed in, "So, living with Mama made you this wise, Papa?"

Sanjay glanced at his daughter, smiling. "Absolutely. You know, Chitra, it's not about one moment or one person. It's about a series of life experiences—everything that has happened over the years. But especially all through these years of marriage. Your mother has been my partner through it all, and we've learned together. It's not always been easy, but every lesson came from the life we've built."

Sujata raised an eyebrow, pretending to be serious. "Good answer, Mr. Wise Papa. I'll make sure you remember that every time you're giving out life lessons."

Chitra burst into laughter, watching the light-hearted banter between her parents.

Sanjay continued, his voice soft but filled with reflection. "It's the journey—every moment we've lived together—that's shaped who I am today. The challenges, the little victories, the struggles—they all taught me things no one else could. Especially your mother. Together, we've built this life and learned how to navigate it side by side."

Sujata smiled softly, her teasing replaced with a quiet warmth. "Well, at least you're finally giving credit where it's due."

Sanjay laughed, nodding. "Yes, absolutely. No need to look back too far. Everything I know now, everything I am now, is because of the life we've built—together."

Chitra looked between her parents, her heart swelling with warmth. She could see the deep connection they shared, and the understanding that life's real wisdom comes from living it—side by side with the people who matter the most.

As the stars began to fill the sky and the park grew quieter, the playful banter settled into a comfortable silence. For Chitra, this moment was a lesson in itself—about love, partnership, and the importance of learning from life's experiences as a family. She looked up at her father, her expression thoughtful. "So... you and Mama had to figure out all this together?"

Sanjay smiled gently. "Yes, we did. And we're still learning, every day. But that's what a good relationship is, Chitra—it's a journey of growth. And the most important part of that journey is making sure that both partners feel cherished and needed. That's what keeps the relationship strong."

He paused, letting his words sink in.

"Success and failure, in relationships or in life," he added, "they come and go. Don't get too attached to either. What really matters is the growth, the journey you're on. Whether it's your career, your relationships, or your personal goals—don't identify with success or failure. Both are temporary. What's important is that you keep moving forward, learning, and growing."

"You know, Chitra," Sanjay began, his voice steady and calm, "failure isn't the end of the road. It's just a part of the journey. The only time you truly fail is when you stop trying." Chitra looked up at him, still searching for understanding.

"I've faced many setbacks in my life," he continued. "But each time, I learned that you've got to get up and keep moving. Every challenge is an opportunity to grow stronger, smarter, and better prepared for the next step. What matters is not how many times you fall, but how many times you get back up."

Chitra nodded slowly, absorbing her father's words. He smiled warmly at her and said, "Remember this: failure is just one stop on the way to success. You learn, you grow, and then you try again... because there is always a next time!"

The stars were twinkling brighter in the sky now, the park almost empty as families began to head home. But for Sanjay and Chitra, the evening felt full of meaning, each word carrying the weight of experience and wisdom.

Chitra turned to her father, her voice soft. "I understand, Papa. I'll remember everything."

Sanjay continued, his voice filled with love and warmth, "You know, Chitra, everything your mother and I have built, all the sacrifices, the long nights, and the hard decisions—it's all been for you. We wanted to give you the foundation to live your life freely, to make your own choices. But always remember, none of this would have been possible without your mother's unwavering strength and love." He paused, glancing at Sujata again, feeling a deep gratitude for the life they had shared together.

As they observed some people in the distance walking along the park's winding path, the cool evening air felt soothing against their faces. Sanjay glanced at Chitra, noticing the thoughtful expression on her face. He knew that growing up meant learning not just about the world outside, but also about the complex emotions within the people closest to you.

"Chitra," Sanjay began gently, "there's something important I want you to remember, especially when it comes to your mother."

Chitra looked up at him, her curiosity piqued.

"Sometimes," Sanjay continued, "when your mother is stressed, she might seem upset or even angry at you, or even me! She might say things that feel harsh, but I want you to understand something—it's not always about us. It's because she's dealing with her own pain or stress. When people are in pain, either physically or emotionally, they sometimes express it in ways that seem hard. But that doesn't change how much she loves you. In fact, she loves you more than anything else in this world."

Chitra listened carefully, a small frown creasing her forehead. "Does that mean I should just ignore when she's upset?" she asked.

Sanjay smiled. "No, beta. You don't ignore it, but you don't take it personally either. When you see someone you love is in pain, whether it's your mother, a friend, or even a teacher at school, try to stay calm. Don't react with anger or frustration. Instead, understand that their harsh words are just an expression of their own pain. Your job is to be patient, to do what needs to be done at that moment. You'll notice that, once the storm passes, they'll appreciate your understanding."

Chitra nodded slowly, digesting her father's words.

"It's the same in school too," Sanjay continued. "Sometimes your teacher might scold you or others for no obvious reason. It may feel unfair, but it's likely because they are dealing with stress you can't see. In those moments, just stay calm and do what's needed. It's not easy, but it's a life experience that will help you for the rest of your life."

Chitra smiled, feeling a sense of clarity and warmth in her father's guidance. "I understand, Papa. I'll try to remember that."

Sanjay gave her a gentle pat on the shoulder, pleased that his daughter was grasping these subtle but important truths. The world around them seemed peaceful, and as they walked further into the night, Sanjay felt comforted, knowing that Chitra was growing into someone who could navigate life's complexities with empathy and wisdom.

Chitra's face softened, her eyes reflecting a quiet understanding and a newfound appreciation for the wisdom her father was sharing.

Sanjay smiled, feeling a deep sense of peace. He stood, offering his hand to Chitra, and together they walked over to join Sujata on the mat. As they again sat down together, the night sky stretching above them, Sanjay felt grateful. He had shared important life experiences with his daughter—life experiences about relationships, about growth, about the importance of communication and understanding. And as they enjoyed their snack, he knew that these life experiences would guide Chitra as she stepped into her future.

Sanjay leaned back, a playful smile spreading across his face. He had been sharing life experiences with Chitra for most of the evening, but he knew it was time for a lighter moment. "Chitra," he said, his tone light but instructive, "let me tell you a funny little story—about a father, a son, and a donkey."

Sanjay smiled as Chitra smirked knowingly. "I know, Papa," she interrupted with a grin, "the donkey story. You've told me that before!"

Sanjay chuckled. "Alright, alright, smart one. Then you already know the point I'm about to make."

Chitra leaned back, folding her arms, playful yet attentive. "You mean, don't react before understanding the full picture?"

"Exactly," Sanjay nodded. "Life will throw opinions and situations at you from all directions. People will say things, often without knowing all the facts, and it's easy to jump to conclusions. But remember, if you react to every passing judgment, you'll end up like that poor father—carrying the donkey. Think about school, for example. There will always be people—whether teachers, classmates, or even friends—who will have opinions about how you should act, study, or even who you should be friends with. If you try to react to every single opinion or bend to every expectation, you'll end up losing your way. It's just like that story of the father and the donkey: if you try to please everyone, you'll find yourself weighed down by other people's judgments. Whether it's a teacher's opinion about your abilities or a friend's passing remark, you need to understand when to take advice and when to stay true to yourself. Learn to process things, take a step back when needed, like that rubber band I mentioned earlier. And remember, just like waves, emotions and opinions will come and go. Your strength lies in knowing when to ride the wave and when to let it pass."

Chitra laughed, nodding. "Got it, Papa. I'll think before I react."

Sanjay gave her a proud look. "Good. Just remember, life is less about responding to every comment and more about taking the time to understand before making a move. Once you learn to move past the noise and distractions of what others say, you'll find a clear path ahead, filled with your own choices—not driven by others' opinions, but by your own clarity of thought."

Chitra gave a gentle nod, seeing the depth of wisdom and understanding in her father's eyes.

The evening air was cool now, but the warmth between them—between father, mother, and daughter—was unmistakable. **As they sat together under the wide open sky, Sanjay felt certain that Chitra would carry these life experiences with her, navigating her own journey with the wisdom and understanding that had taken him a lifetime to learn.**

ꕥꕥꕥ

My Top 10 Learnings:

1. **Navigating Distractions**: Sanjay reflects on how distractions, especially during his teenage years, impacted his focus and priorities. He shares that distractions can be both appealing and deceptive, pulling one away from meaningful goals.

2. **Value of Focus**: The chapter emphasizes the importance of staying focused on long-term goals. Sanjay explains how losing sight of his dreams temporarily delayed his progress and how he later realized the value of clarity in decision-making.

3. **Learning from Relationships**: Sanjay candidly discusses past relationships and how they initially seemed important but ultimately served as distractions. He underscores the lesson that not all relationships contribute positively to personal growth.

4. **True Love vs. Apparent Attraction**: A key distinction Sanjay makes is between true love and mere external attraction. He highlights the depth of commitment, communication, and resilience that real love requires, contrasting it with fleeting infatuations.

5. **Commitment and Growth**: The chapter teaches that real relationships are built on mutual support and growth. Sanjay appreciates how his partnership with Chitra's mother, Sujata, helped him grow personally and professionally, demonstrating the power of supportive relationships.

6. **Clarity in Purpose**: Sanjay emphasizes that clarity in one's purpose and values is critical. Without it, distractions can easily pull individuals away from their true path.

7. **Building Emotional Resilience**: Sanjay teaches Chitra that resilience—both emotional and mental—is essential to navigate life's ups and downs, particularly

when distractions and temptations arise.

8. **Balancing Tradition with Modernity:** Sanjay shares how he and Sujata balanced their traditional values with modern ambitions, teaching Chitra the importance of maintaining one's identity while evolving with the times.

9. **Learning from Mistakes:** The chapter encourages embracing mistakes as valuable life lessons. Sanjay admits to being distracted in the past but stresses that those experiences ultimately guided him toward clarity and growth.

10. **Wisdom in Retrospection:** Sanjay's reflections show how wisdom often comes from looking back on life's choices. He encourages Chitra to learn from his experiences and gain clarity early on, avoiding unnecessary distractions.

3

When I Discovered The True Meaning of Love

Sanjay sat quietly, his thoughts deep and reflective, as he looked out over the calm waters of the lake. The years had given him many experiences, both joyful and challenging, but he was grateful for each one. He had grown from a young man filled with ambition and uncertainty into someone who had found clarity, purpose, and direction. The path he had walked was far from straightforward, yet it was these very twists and turns that shaped his understanding of life. He was now at a place where he could guide Chitra with the wisdom he had earned. His journey had taught him the value of patience, the importance of staying focused on long-term goals, and above all, the significance of family. As he prepared to share more of his life's lessons with Chitra, he felt a sense of fulfilment—knowing that his role as a father was not just to protect, but to prepare her for the road ahead.

Chitra sat on the mat, cross-legged, her fingers absentmindedly tracing patterns on the grass as the evening's quiet settled in around them. The playful energy she had carried throughout her birthday celebration had softened, replaced by a thoughtful stillness. Her wide eyes, bright with curiosity, occasionally darted toward her father, anticipating what would come next in their conversation. She was transitioning, Sanjay realized, moving from the lightness of childhood into the deeper waters of adolescence, where questions about life and love started to take shape in her mind.

They had been sitting on the picnic mat for some time now, with Sujata quietly tending to the last few items from their meal, her presence grounding them as always. But Sanjay could feel that the moment was ripe for something more—something deeper. With a soft smile, he stood up, nodding for Chitra to follow him. She rose and, without a word, walked alongside him toward the wooden bench that faced the serene lake.

As they sat once again on the bench, the moonlight shimmering softly on the water, Sanjay could feel the significance of the moment deepening. The cool breeze brushed against their faces, and the rustling leaves above them provided a gentle, meditative soundtrack to the evening. The stars had begun to scatter across the night sky, casting a calm over the park. It was here, under the soft glow of the moon, that Sanjay knew the time was right to share one of the most important lessons life had taught him: the true meaning of love.

He turned toward Chitra, his voice gentle, but filled with the importance of what he was about to say. "Chitra," he began, "we've talked a lot today about life, distractions, and goals. But there's something I've been thinking about recently—something that I wish I had known earlier."

Chitra looked up at her father, her expression curious, sensing that this wasn't going to be like the other conversations they had shared until now.

Sanjay turned to the side, glancing towards Sujata, who was still seated on the mat. He paused for a moment, his thoughts drifting to the past seventeen years they had shared—filled with ups, downs, and countless moments of growth. A warm, thankful smile spread across his face as he reflected on the quiet strength she had always been, the anchor in his life. Then, with a gentle exhale, he turned back to Chitra, his heart full of love and pride.

Sujata glanced over at him, her eyes warm with appreciation for the life experiences Sanjay was imparting to Chitra. She smiled gently, her expression a reflection of quiet pride, recognizing the wisdom he was sharing. It was moments like these that reaffirmed the bond they had built over the years, their shared responsibility of guiding Chitra through the intricacies of life.

Sanjay smiled faintly, gathering his thoughts before speaking again to Chitra. "Choosing a life partner is one of the most important decisions you'll ever make. It's a choice that affects not just your life but the lives of future generations. And there are things I've learned—things that have become clearer as I've grown older—that I want to share with you."

He could see the curiosity in Chitra's eyes as she waited for him to continue.

"One of the most important life experiences I've learned," Sanjay said softly, "is that choosing a partner who shares the same cultural, social, linguistic, and economic background can bring long-term benefits. These are things that might not seem important at first, but they create a foundation for a strong, harmonious relationship."

Chitra tilted her head slightly, listening intently. "Why is that so important, Papa?"

Sanjay's smile deepened, and he looked out at the lake, recalling his own journey. "Let's start with cultural compatibility. When you share the same cultural background with your partner, you share traditions, values, and expectations. It's more than just celebrating the same festivals or following the same customs—it's about understanding each other on a deeper level. When you both have a similar worldview, there's less room for misunderstanding, and you can raise your children with a strong sense of identity and continuity."

He paused for a moment, letting that sink in before continuing. "For example," Sanjay continued, "although your mother and I are from different geographical regions of Bengal, we both grew up in almost identical Bengali households. The values, the traditions, and the way family shaped our lives—it was all very similar. That's why, despite our different backgrounds, we could build a life together with such understanding. We understood the importance of family traditions, the role of elders, and the way we wanted to raise you. That common understanding created a foundation of respect and mutual expectations that helped us avoid conflicts, especially in the early years of our marriage."

Chitra nodded, understanding what her father meant. She had seen how smoothly her parents navigated family traditions and how they always seemed to be on the same page when it came to important decisions.

"And then," Sanjay added, "there's the importance of language. Our mother tongue, even with its different dialects, creates a deep connection. Sharing the same mother tongue fosters clear communication, not just in words, but in understanding the deeper nuances of emotion, culture, and tradition. It's something that bridges even the smallest gaps between two people. We express love, humour, and even resolve conflicts differently in our native language. It's not just about the words—it's about the emotional connection that comes with them. Your mother and I could speak freely, without misunderstandings, because we shared that linguistic bond. It's a gift you pass down to your children, allowing them to connect with their heritage and their identity."

Chitra looked thoughtful, realizing the importance of language in ways she hadn't before. She had always taken for granted that her parents communicated so effortlessly, but now she understood how deeply that shaped their relationship.

Sanjay's voice grew a little more serious as he shifted to the next point. "Another thing that's often overlooked is the importance of shared social and economic backgrounds. When partners come from similar economic situations, they tend to have similar expectations about money, lifestyle, and the future. This helps avoid misunderstandings or conflicts related to finances, which can be one of the biggest strains on a marriage."

He paused, glancing at Chitra. "It's not about wealth, Chitra. It's about how you approach money, savings, and your future goals. Your mother and I both came from families where financial stability was valued. We knew the importance of saving for the future, of planning for your education, and of building a life based on shared financial values. That alignment brought us closer and made it easier for us to work toward our goals."

Chitra nodded, her face serious. She had seen how carefully her parents managed their finances, ensuring that she had everything she needed while planning for the future.

Sanjay leaned forward slightly, his voice quieter now. "And then there's the matter of emotional compatibility. When you and your partner come from a similar age group," he paused for emphasis, "and by age group, I mean to say that girls grow more mentally mature than boys of the same age. So, you should consider that when deciding. But beyond that, having similar socio-economic backgrounds can also make a big difference. It means you're more likely to be on the same page emotionally. You'll have shared life experiences, understandings, and priorities, which makes it much easier to meet each other's needs and support each other's growth."

He sighed softly, reflecting on his own past. "In my early relationships, I didn't understand this, Chitra. I used to think that love was enough. But back then, love meant something different to me—more like a superficial attraction. It wasn't until later that I realized real emotional needs run deeper than just feelings of romance. Men and women communicate differently, and if you don't take the time to understand that, misunderstandings are bound to happen."

He paused, then added gently, "I want you to find someone who doesn't just listen to your words but understands you in those silent, unspoken moments. That's what real emotional connection looks like, and it's so much more important than just superficial attraction."

Chitra listened closely, her gaze never leaving her father's face.

Sanjay smiled softly, continuing, "Your mother and I learned early on that we needed to respect each other's space and emotional needs. There were times when I needed to withdraw, to process things alone, and she respected that. And there were times when she needed closeness, and I learned to be there for her. It's a balance, but one that's important to get right."

He shifted in his seat, his voice taking on a more reflective tone. "In the long run, when you and your partner share these things—culture, language, financial goals, emotional understanding—you create a foundation for a stable, harmonious relationship. And that foundation isn't just for you. It's something that will shape the lives of your children and the generations that come after."

Chitra looked up at him, her eyes wide with understanding. "It's about more than just the two people in the relationship," she said quietly.

Sanjay nodded. "Exactly. It's about the family you build together, the values you pass down to your children. When you and your partner are aligned in these ways, your children grow up in a stable environment. They learn the importance of cultural traditions, the value of financial wisdom, and the strength that comes from emotional compatibility."

He paused, letting his words settle into the quiet of the night. "Chitra," he said softly, "love is important—of course, it is. But you need to understand what love really means. Love is not just a feeling of passion. Love is a commitment, it's a choice you make every day. Love is selfless service in real life, it's about showing up for each other, even when it's hard."

His voice deepened with conviction as he added, "Choosing a partner who shares these values with you will give you a stronger foundation. It's not just about romance; it's about building something together that will last. This choice you make will shape not only your future but also the legacy you leave behind, for the generations to come."

Chitra sat quietly, absorbing the weight of her father's words, the evening wrapping them in its stillness. She nodded, her mind filled with the wisdom her father had shared. "Thank you, Papa," she said softly, her voice filled with gratitude.

Sanjay smiled, his heart swelling with pride. He knew that the life experiences he had shared today would guide her for years to come, shaping not just her future, but the future of the family she would one day build.

While the soft evening breeze swirled around the park, carrying with it the faint scent of jasmine, Sanjay and Chitra got up and began walking once again. Their footsteps were slow, thoughtful, as they followed the illuminated pathway toward the lakefront. The distant hum of the city seemed to fade as the peaceful ambiance of the park enveloped them, with the shimmering water reflecting the gentle glow of the surrounding lights. The quiet offered them a sanctuary, a space to let the weight of their conversation settle, as they continued their walk side by side, lost in thought.

The conversations of the evening had already deepened into relationships, responsibilities, and family legacies, but there was still something pressing on Sanjay's mind. Something important he had to explain to his daughter—a concept that he knew, if understood correctly, could shape her entire approach to life.

Sanjay paused for a moment, gathering his thoughts. "Chitra," he began slowly, "we've talked a lot about choosing the right life partner, haven't we? About finding someone who shares your values, your vision, and your history. But there's something deeper I need you to understand about this."

Chitra looked at her father, her curiosity piqued by the weight of his tone.

"You see," Sanjay continued, "in today's world, a lot of people dismiss the idea of caste and family lineage as something old-fashioned. Some people even think of it as an evil system, one that divides people. You may hear this from your friends or even read about it in many places. But I want you to hear this from me—there's more to it than what meets the eye."

Chitra's expression remained attentive, her father's words flowing over her with a calm authority. She trusted him deeply, knowing that his wisdom came not from prejudice, but from a place of deep understanding and life experience of over four decades.

"Our surnames, are our traditions—they carry thousands of years of history. They are not just labels or categories," Sanjay explained, his voice steady. "They represent generations of families who contributed to society in meaningful ways. The caste system, in its original form, wasn't about division. It was about organizing society so that everyone could play a role that benefited the greater good."

Chitra nodded, trying to absorb this broader perspective. She had heard conflicting ideas about caste from her peers, but this was the first time she truly understood the depth behind it.

"Take our surname, Chakrabarti, for example," Sanjay continued. "It means 'leader' or 'ruler of the country' or 'emperor.' For centuries, the Chakrabarties have been known as the best scholars, top of the line religious guides, and leaders in their community. It's not just a name; it's a legacy. And it comes with responsibility—responsibility to uphold the values that have been passed down to us—something we can be seriously proud of."

He glanced at Chitra to see how she was taking it in, and seeing her thoughtful expression, he pressed on. "The same goes for other surnames—Chatterjee, Banerjee, Mukherjee, Bhattacharjee, Ganguly. These families are part of the Kulin Brahmins, the highest tier of Bengali Brahmins. They've been intellectual leaders, priests, and educators for centuries. These names aren't just identifiers; they're symbols of families who have contributed to the cultural and intellectual development of Bengal for generations."

Chitra's eyes widened with understanding as Sanjay elaborated further. "Chatterjee, for instance, were part of the highly respected Kulin Brahmin families from the village of Chattagram, now in modern-day Bangladesh. They weren't just ordinary families—they were considered intellectual and spiritual leaders, revered for their contributions to education and religious practices. For centuries, they played key roles in religious rituals, education, and the preservation of knowledge. Banerjees, another Kulin Brahmin surname, have long been involved in literature and philosophy, shaping our intellectual traditions. And the Mukherjees—well, they've been crucial in preserving the cultural and religious fabric of Bengal. These aren't just names, Chitra. They are legacies, passed down through hundreds or even thousands of generations."

Chitra was silent for a moment, absorbing the weight of her father's words. "But Papa," she asked softly, "what about people who say caste is just a way of creating divisions?"

Sanjay smiled gently. "That's a fair question," he said. "And yes, there were times when people misused the caste system for their own gain, and that caused divisions. But that wasn't the original purpose. The caste system was designed to create balance in society, ensuring that everyone had a role to play. Our surnames, remind us of the roles our ancestors played—the responsibilities they carried for their communities."

He paused, his voice softening as he added, "What I want you to remember, Chitra, is that when the time comes for you to choose a life partner, it's not just about love. It's about joining two legacies. When you marry someone who shares your cultural background, your values, your history, you're not just creating a union between two individuals. You're building a family on strong, shared foundations. It ensures that your children grow up with a deep understanding of who they are, and where they come from."

Chitra looked thoughtful, her mind turning over everything her father had said. "So, it's not about thinking we're better than anyone else," she said slowly, "it's about understanding where we come from, and carrying that forward."

"Exactly," Sanjay replied, pride in his voice. "It's about continuity. It's about knowing that you are part of something bigger than yourself. And when you marry someone from a similar background, who respects that history, you build something strong—something that will last for generations."

He continued, drawing in the quiet night around them. "Think about the other surnames we're connected to—Bagchi, Bhaduri, Goswami, Ghoshal, Lahiri, Maitra, Sanyal. Each of these families has played a role in shaping our society. Bagchis have long been connected to religious practices, Bhaduris were scholars, Goswamis were custodians of temples, and Ghoshals were known for their contributions to philosophy and law. Each surname carries with it a story, a legacy. And when you understand and respect that, you're not just building a life—you're building a future grounded in history."

Chitra smiled, understanding now what her father had been trying to tell her. "So, when the time comes to choose a partner, it's not just about what we want now. It's about thinking of the future, thinking about what we'll build together."

"Exactly," Sanjay said warmly. "It's about ensuring that your family—our family—has a strong foundation. And remember, Chitra, this isn't about superiority or hierarchy. It's about continuity, about carrying forward the values and traditions that have shaped our family for so many generations."

As Sanjay spoke, he paused, his voice soft and thoughtful. "Chitra, as we talk about family, traditions, and surnames, it's important you understand something crucial. While I've shared with you the significance of our own heritage and the values that come with it, that doesn't mean I see other backgrounds or castes as any less important. Every family, every surname, carries its own history, its own contributions to society, their own way. Just as our family has a legacy in education and culture, other families have theirs in other different fields—be it art, business, craftsmanship, or service. I deeply respect that, and I hope that in every family, they should respect their own lineage and their own different values are continued and celebrated, no matter what profession they follow. What matters most is that we all take pride in who we are and where we come from, while also respecting others and the diversity that makes our world so rich and vibrant."

Chitra nodded, feeling a sense of pride in her heritage that she hadn't fully understood before—something which not even the school teaches her correctly!

As they continued walking, the stars twinkling brightly above them, Sanjay knew that Chitra's understanding of her place in the world had deepened. She now saw herself not just as an individual, but as part of a long, unbroken chain of history—a legacy that she would one day pass on to her own children.

And in that moment, as the cool evening breeze whispered around them, Sanjay felt a quiet sense of fulfilment settle deep within him. He realized he had given Chitra something beyond any worldly possession—a profound understanding of her identity, her roots, and the legacy she was entrusted to carry forward. It was a gift woven with the threads of heritage, values, and the responsibility to preserve and build upon the foundation set by their ancestors.

As their conversation drifted into the quiet night, Sanjay's thoughts turned to his own journey through life, especially the bond he had shared with Sujata. He knew there was one more life experience, an essential one about marriage and companionship, that he needed to impart to his daughter. His gaze softened as he reflected on his own path with Sujata, a partnership that had weathered life's challenges and joys alike.

"Chitra," he began, "Marriage isn't just about two people falling in love and building a life together. In our Indian context, it's the union of two families—two sets of histories, traditions, and expectations. When your mother and I got married, we didn't just become husband and wife; we became part of each other's families. And that's something people often overlook."

He smiled, thinking about Sujata. "Your mother has this incredible ability to balance things. She didn't just marry me; she embraced my family—your grandparents, aunts, uncles—with open arms, even when it wasn't always easy. It's not that relationships with in-laws are always challenging, but they come with their own set of expectations and dynamics. And in our culture, that can sometimes be very demanding."

He leaned back, his tone thoughtful. "You know how independent and driven your mother is. She has always been academically focused, managing a highly successful career. But when it came to our family, she never let that take a back seat. She handled any tensions that arose with grace—whether it was small misunderstandings with your grandparents or the expectations that came with being part of a traditional Bengali family. Your mother knew how to respect those traditions without losing herself in them."

Sanjay's voice grew softer as he continued, "And through it all, she made sure you were raised with love, understanding, and patience. She balanced the old with the new, the traditional values of our families with the modern mind-set we wanted to instil in you. And that balance, Chitra, is what has made our family strong."

He smiled warmly at his daughter. "Marriage, in our context, is a lifelong partnership, not just between two individuals, but between two families. Your mother taught me that love, respect, and understanding are the pillars that hold that partnership strong. It's not always easy, but when two people support each other through life's ups and downs, it creates something far more meaningful than just love alone."

Chitra nodded thoughtfully, absorbing his words. "I understand, Papa," she said in a quiet voice, the depth of the life experience settling in. "It's about more than just being in love—it's about building something lasting with respect and commitment."

As the night deepened around them, Sanjay felt a deep sense of peace. **He had passed on a gift that would last far beyond this moment—a gift of understanding, of wisdom, and of love that would echo through generations.**

ϷϷϷ

My Top 10 Learnings:

1. **Love as a Foundation of Support**: Sanjay emphasizes that true love is not just about superficial romantic attraction but is rooted in being a consistent support system for each other through life's ups and downs.
2. **Mutual Respect and Understanding**: Sanjay explains that genuine love grows when both partners respect each other's individuality and create a safe space for expression.
3. **Patience in Love**: Love is not about rushing into any random relationship or expecting immediate perfection. Sanjay shares how patience, understanding each other's pace, and allowing growth strengthen the bond.

4. **Emotional Maturity:** True love requires emotional maturity, where partners understand and accept each other's vulnerabilities, creating a deeper connection.

5. **Love as a Choice:** Sanjay teaches Chitra that love is a deliberate choice made daily. It's about choosing to care, nurture, and invest in the relationship despite life's challenges.

6. **Selfless Love:** Sanjay highlights that real love is not transactional—it's about selflessly giving to your partner without expecting anything in return, knowing that this shared generosity is what sustains the relationship.

7. **Love Requires Balance:** Sanjay reflects on the importance of balancing personal goals and ambitions with the needs of the relationship, ensuring that both partners grow together without losing their individual identities.

8. **Conflict Resolution through Love:** Love does not mean avoiding conflict; rather, it's about handling disagreements with respect, compassion, and a desire to understand each other.

9. **Celebrating Differences:** Sanjay emphasizes that true love celebrates differences between partners. It's these differences that enrich the relationship, rather than being points of contention.

10. **Legacy of Love:** Sanjay points out that love is about leaving behind a legacy. A healthy, loving relationship sets an example for future generations, showing what it means to truly care for and support one another.

4

Where I Found Passion In My Profession

"*Balancing your work and family means knowing when to step back, stay present, and trust that love, patience, and understanding create a stronger, happier home, because it's not about you being perfect, but about you being there.*"

- Sujata

Sujata moved with quiet grace as she arranged some remnants of their picnic, her actions calm and unhurried. Sanjay watched her, feeling a wave of appreciation for the role she played in their lives. She wasn't just a partner—she was the bedrock of their family, the silent strength that kept everything and everyone grounded. Her presence brought a sense of peace, a quiet assurance that no matter how hectic life became, she would always be there, steady and strong. Sanjay admired the way she balanced everything so effortlessly, whether it was managing the household, supporting him in his pursuits, or nurturing Chitra as she grew. In moments like these, he realized just how much he depended on her unwavering support and quiet wisdom, qualities that had shaped their family's bond. Sujata wasn't just his companion; she was the heart of their journey together.

Sanjay leaned back slightly on the bench, the wooden slats cool beneath him as the night deepened around Eco Park. The stars, now fully awake in the sky, twinkled brightly above, their light reflecting softly on the still waters of the lake. The evening breeze carried a refreshing coolness, gently brushing against his face and filling the quiet space between him and his daughter.

He glanced at Chitra, who sat beside him, her legs swinging lightly, her eyes fixed on the shimmering water. It was one of those moments when time seemed to stretch out, offering a rare stillness in the whirlwind of life. He could sense that she was ready—ready to hear the next part of his journey, one filled with purpose and passion.

The conversation they had started earlier lingered in the air, and Sanjay felt the weight of the stories he was about to tell. His thoughts travelled back to his early years, a time when the distractions of youth had faded, making way for a deeper understanding of what truly mattered to him. Now was the time to share that with Chitra.

As the cool breeze gently caressed their faces, Sanjay gathered his thoughts. He was about to impart one of the most important lessons life had taught him—the moment he discovered his passion in his profession and how that passion shaped his life.

The weight of the conversation had grown, but there was a calmness in the air—a moment suspended in time—a rare stillness amidst the busyness of everyday life, as Sanjay mentally gathered together, some of the most important life experiences of his life, for his daughter.

Chitra, having crossed the threshold of childhood into her teenage years, was ready for these life experiences, and Sanjay could sense her openness to receive them. He looked at her thoughtfully, knowing how important this time was. The calmness of the park mirrored the calmness in his heart, as if the universe had paused to allow him this opportunity to guide his daughter. It was more than just a father-daughter conversation; it was a passing of wisdom, a chance to share the most important values, ones that would carry Chitra forward into her own life. The breeze brushed lightly across their faces, carrying with it a sense of clarity, as if nature itself was part of this quiet, reflective exchange.

Sanjay, feeling the deep connection between them, prepared to offer the life experiences that had shaped him—life experiences that would now shape his daughter's path ahead. He looked over at Chitra, the faint glow of the moon casting soft light on her face. He could see that she was processing everything they had discussed, and he knew this was the right moment to leave her with another important thought for the evening. "Chitra," Sanjay began, his voice soft but firm, "everything we've been talking about today has led to this moment. You've turned thirteen, and I want you to understand something very important. You need to take charge of your life. No one else is going to do it for you."

Chitra looked at him, her wide eyes attentive, sensing the seriousness in her father's tone. Sanjay took a deep breath, knowing how vital this life experience was.

"Life isn't going to hand you success or happiness on a platter," he continued. "You need to shape your own path. Personal responsibility is one of the most important things you'll ever learn. It's easy to blame external circumstances when things go wrong, but you have the power to take control. You can choose how to respond, how to move forward, and how to build your future."

Chitra nodded slowly, absorbing her father's words.

Sanjay smiled gently, his eyes twinkling with a mix of wisdom and warmth. "This is why I've always been careful about where I invest my time and energy. It's important to invest in assets, not liabilities. When I started my architectural business, I wasn't just thinking about the present. I was thinking about creating something that would grow in value over time—something that would last. I want you to do the same, Chitra."

Chitra tilted her head, curiosity filling her voice. "What do you mean, Papa?"

"Assets," Sanjay explained, "are things that put money into your pocket, things that generate value. They're not just for momentary pleasure. They're investments in your future. For me, it was architecture. It wasn't just a job; it was a way of building something meaningful, something that could provide for our family long after I'm gone. And that's what I want for you. Whatever path you choose—personal or professional—make sure you're investing in things that will help you grow: physically, mentally, and financially."

Chitra nodded, her eyes focused, absorbing the weight of her father's words.

"Chitra," Sanjay continued, his tone calm yet serious, "there's something crucial about money that most people don't understand. People earn money and think it's for buying things they want—cars, gadgets, clothes. While it feels good in the moment, there's a smarter way to use that money."

Intrigued, Chitra leaned in closer, eager for more.

Sanjay smiled. "I learned this late in life, and I had to struggle because of it. But I want you to learn it early. Don't waste your money on liabilities first. Instead, buy assets. You know why?"

Chitra shook her head.

"Because assets put money into your pocket. They work for you, generating income. Liabilities, on the other hand, take money out of your pocket," he explained patiently. "Think of an asset like a rental property, stocks, or a business—things that generate income. Liabilities are things like cars or gadgets that lose value and cost you more in the long run. Most people buy liabilities first, then wonder why they're always struggling to save."

Chitra nodded, starting to understand the bigger picture.

"Here's the secret," Sanjay said, his voice gaining a quiet intensity. "Invest your money in assets first. Let those assets create a cash flow for you. Once you have a steady stream of income from those assets, then—and only then—should you think about buying liabilities. Want a new phone? A new car? Fine, but let your assets pay for it. Don't drain your savings or take out a bad loan that becomes a burden."

Chitra's eyes lit up with understanding. "So, it's like... using money to make more money first?"

"Exactly," Sanjay said, his smile widening. "That's how you build wealth over time. You create a system where your assets generate cash, and you use that cash flow to fund your wants. You never dip into your savings or paycheck for things that don't grow in value."

Sanjay paused, gazing out at the bustling streets and distant city lights. "This is something most people don't get.

They buy liabilities first because they want to look successful, to show off to their friends or family. But in reality, they're chaining themselves financially. You, Chitra, should aim for financial freedom because it's only through financial freedom that you'll have the ability to pursue what you truly love in life—without limitations."

Chitra smiled softly, the weight of her father's words settling into her heart. "I get it, Papa. Buy assets first, let them pay for the things I want later."

Sanjay nodded, proud of his daughter's grasp of this essential principle. "Yes. When you live like this, you won't just have what you want—you'll have the peace of mind that comes with financial security. That's the real power of building assets first."

They both chuckled lightly, feeling the ease of a shared understanding. Sitting on the park bench overlooking the lake, with the faint glow of city lights reflecting on the water, the conversation took on a lighter tone. Sanjay leaned back, his eyes twinkling. "You know, when I was your age, I wanted a flashy video game console or a Walkman. But I quickly learned that you can't buy everything the moment you want it. It's like wanting to eat dessert before you've even cooked the meal."

Chitra chuckled at the metaphor. "So, no impulse buying?"

Sanjay shook his head, still smiling. "Not quite. It's not about depriving yourself of nice things, but you need to first invest in assets before you spend on 'wants'. It's about making sure that what you spend on today isn't something that will just drain your pocket. If you're constantly buying things that give you nothing in return, you'll always feel like you're running in place."

"Like what?" Chitra asked.

"Take cars, for example," Sanjay said, gesturing toward the distant cityscape. "Many people spend their entire savings on a brand-new car, but what happens? It loses value quickly. Meanwhile, if you invested that same money in stocks or property, it would grow, and in a few years, you could afford that car without touching your savings."

Chitra listened closely, realizing that her father wasn't just talking about money. He was talking about building a life where your finances work for you, not against you.

"Let's say you want the latest phone," Sanjay continued. "Instead of buying it outright, invest in something like a mutual fund or a small business. When that grows, it can cover the cost of the phone. That way, your money works for you."

Chitra grinned. "So, basically, I have to be smart about how I spend."

"Yes," Sanjay said warmly. "It's about using the fruits of your investments for your wants, not the other way around. That's how you break the cycle of paycheck-to-paycheck living."

As they both looked out at the lights of Kolkata in the distance, Chitra reflected on the wisdom her father had shared. It wasn't just about money—it was about building a life, a future, where she was in control of her destiny. And equipped with her father's life experiences, she knew she was well on her way.

"Time," Sanjay continued, "is even more valuable than money. Once it's gone, you can't get it back. That's why you need to be wise about how you spend it. Money can be earned, lost, and regained, but time doesn't work that way. Don't waste it on things that don't bring you meaning or purpose."

He looked at his daughter, wanting her to truly grasp the importance of this life experience. "Use your time to build something worthwhile—whether it's your career, your relationships, or your passions. And when it comes to money, make sure you're using it wisely too. Money isn't everything, but it's a tool that can help you live a life filled with meaning. Don't let it control you—learn how to control it."

Chitra nodded again, her gaze thoughtful as she processed her father's advice.

"And one more thing," Sanjay said, his voice quiet but firm. "Never rely on just one source of income. It's too risky. I've learned that having multiple sources of income is the key to financial security. When you depend on just one job, or just one gig, or just one business, you're vulnerable. That's why I built my architectural business and a couple of other ventures on the side while still working full-time. It gave me the freedom to take risks without fear of losing everything."

He smiled, seeing Chitra's interest deepening. "I want you to think about that as you move forward. Whatever career you choose, always find ways to create additional streams of income. Whether it's through investments, side businesses, or entrepreneurial ventures, never rely on just one thing to keep you stable."

Sanjay paused for a moment, gathering his thoughts, then added with a hint of humour, "Let me explain it like this. Imagine a bucket being filled with water. Now, if you have just one tap pouring water in, that's your single income source. If that tap slows down or stops, what happens to your bucket? It stays empty, right?"

Chitra nodded, following along.

"Now," Sanjay continued, "think of multiple taps filling the bucket—these are your additional streams of income. Each tap represents another source, whether it's an investment, a small business, or even a side gig. The more taps you have, the faster and more reliably your bucket fills up."

Chitra grinned, starting to see where this was going.

"But here's the twist," Sanjay said with a smile. "There are also holes at the bottom of the bucket—these represent expenses. The more liabilities you take on, like buying things you don't need or indulging in lifestyle upgrades that don't add value, the more holes get drilled into the bottom of that bucket. You'll be losing water just as fast as you're filling it, or even faster."

Chitra's smile faded slightly as she absorbed the analogy.

"The key," Sanjay added, "is balance. You have to reduce the urge of drilling so many holes with unnecessary expenses and focus on adding more taps to fill the bucket. That's how you make sure the water—your money—keeps flowing and doesn't run out."

Chitra laughed softly. "So, basically, stop making holes and keep turning on more taps?"

"Exactly," Sanjay chuckled. "Don't drain yourself with more and more liabilities, and instead, keep finding ways to generate more income streams. That way, you'll always have a full bucket, no matter what risk life throws at you."

Chitra's eyes were wide as she absorbed these life experiences, understanding for the first time the importance of financial independence and security.

"And speaking of risks," Sanjay added, his voice softening, "don't be afraid to take them—but take smart ones. Stability is important, yes, but sometimes you have to take a leap of faith to grow. Just make sure it's a calculated risk. We all need some amount of stability, but growth comes from pushing yourself beyond your comfort zone. You'll need to find that balance in life—between taking risks and staying grounded."

The night air whispered through the trees as Sanjay leaned back, a contemplative look in his eyes. He knew Chitra had a long road ahead, and he wanted her to have the skills she needed to navigate it.

As the gentle breeze from Eco Park began to cool, Sanjay glanced over at Chitra, sensing the perfect moment to share another valuable life experience. This one wasn't just about time or focus, but about managing her future in a way that would ensure her financial independence. He had developed a simple method for her to easily grasp how to handle money, a tool she could carry with her always—whether she earned a small amount or much more in the future.

"Chitra," he began softly, his tone a mix of seriousness and warmth, "I've always told you that being financially independent is one of the most important things you can achieve. It's not just about having enough money to live comfortably, but knowing how to manage whatever you have."

Chitra looked up, intrigued. Her father had a knack for making complex things seem simple.

"I call it the 'Crab Claws' method," Sanjay explained, holding up both of his hands in the shape of a claw with his fingers spread out. "This is a simple hack to manage your money every month, whether you earn ₹100, ₹1,000, or ₹1,00,000. The principle remains the same."

He demonstrated by spreading the fingers of both hands. "Each finger represents 10% of your income. Let's start with your right hand." He wiggled his ring and pinkie fingers together. "These two fingers represent 20% of your income, and that's for your 'needs.' That is for food, shelter, basic utilities—everything you need to survive."

Next, he moved his index and middle fingers, showing Chitra their significance. "These two fingers, also representing 20%, are for your 'wants.' These are things like going out, buying something nice for yourself, a treat—but things that aren't necessary for survival."

He separated his thumb from the rest of his fingers. "Now, your thumb—10%—is for 'emergencies.' This is money you don't touch unless something unexpected happens—a medical emergency, a sudden repair, anything that needs immediate attention."

Sanjay then moved to his left hand. "Your left hand is for investments. Your left thumb—10%—is for gold. This is the safest investment, one that retains its value over time. The index and middle fingers together, another 20%, are for equity—stocks or shares. This is where you take some risks, but the returns can be higher."

Finally, he pointed to his left pinkie and ring fingers. "And these two, also 20%, are for real estate. Whether it's land, a home, or property, it's something solid—something that will grow in value as the years go by."

Chitra was quiet, watching her father's hands, understanding the simple yet profound concept behind the "Crab Claws" method.

"This is just a guideline, Chitra," Sanjay continued. "You'll need to adjust it as you grow, depending on your income and your goals. But if you follow this basic structure, you'll never be caught off guard. You'll have a solid plan to take care of yourself and your future."

Chitra smiled, her mind already playing with the possibilities. "So, this is how you manage money, Papa?"

Sanjay nodded. "This is how I started. And it's helped me stay focused—making sure I don't spend more than I should, investing wisely, and always having something saved for emergencies."

He leaned closer, his tone growing more serious. "Money is just a tool, Chitra. But if you use it well, it gives you freedom. Freedom to do what you love, to live without worry, and to help others."

Chitra looked at her own hands, mimicking the "Crab Claws" gesture. "I'll remember this, Papa."

Sanjay smiled softly, feeling proud of the young woman Chitra was becoming. "I know you will, my girl. And when you follow this, you'll have the time and the resources to build the life you want—just like I've always hoped for you."

As the conversation settled into the quiet hum of the night, Sanjay knew he had given Chitra another tool to navigate her future—one that would serve her for years to come.

The conversation deepened and Sanjay turned to a topic he felt was crucial for Chitra as she entered her teenage years. The quiet strength in his voice became even more focused, as he wanted her to understand not just the complexities of time, but also the importance of protecting herself.

"Chitra, there's something else we need to talk about. It's important that as you grow older, you learn how to defend yourself—not just physically, but mentally and financially too."

Chitra looked up at him, curiosity in her eyes. "Defend myself?"

"Yes, dear," Sanjay replied, "You'll meet many people in life—some with good intentions, and some who may not respect your boundaries. It's essential that you clearly understand make others understand the difference between what is a 'good touch' and a 'bad touch' for you. No one has the right to make you feel uncomfortable. You need to trust your instincts and never be afraid to speak up."

Chitra listened intently as her father continued. "I know it can feel scary, but you must be strong. If anyone ever crosses that line, whether they're a stranger or someone close, you have the right to say no. And if they don't listen, you have to defend yourself—with physical strength and tactics if necessary."

His eyes softened for a moment before growing serious again. "But this goes beyond just physical defence. You need to be strong mentally as well. People may try to manipulate or control you, but you must always remember your worth. Know that your value doesn't come from someone else's opinion of you, but from what you think of yourself."

Chitra nodded, her gaze fixed on her father, absorbing every word.

The late evening had draped Eco Park in a soft, tranquil glow. The sky, now a deep shade of indigo, was dotted with a few scattered stars. The illuminated boats drifted gracefully across the lake, their reflections shimmering like streaks of light on the water. Chitra and Sanjay sat together, watching the spectacle in quiet admiration.

The boats, with their gentle, almost dreamlike movements, seemed to echo the peaceful rhythm of the night. Sanjay glanced at Chitra, noticing how captivated she was by the glowing scene. He smiled softly, taking in the serene moment before speaking.

"Chitra," he began, his voice calm and thoughtful, "look at those boats. They're all different shapes and sizes, yet each one is beautiful in its own way. None of them are trying to outshine the other. They simply are."

Chitra nodded, her eyes still on the boats, their soft glow dancing on the water.

"It's the same with us," Sanjay continued. "We don't need to be like anyone else to be beautiful or worthy. You don't need to change your looks or anything about yourself, not for anyone. Just like these boats, you have your own light. And if someone truly cares for you, they'll love you for who you are, just as you are."

Chitra smiled, feeling the comfort of his words settle in her heart. The illuminated boats seemed to reflect the message, each one gliding effortlessly, confident in its own glow.

"And," Sanjay added, turning his gaze back to the lake, "just like those boats, you need to be self-sufficient. You can navigate the waters of life on your own, without waiting for someone to steer you. Take care of yourself, learn to be independent. It's a strength that will serve you well, no matter what."

The boats drifted past, their lights softening as they moved farther across the lake, and in the quiet of that late evening, Chitra felt something shift within her—an understanding that she was enough, just as she was, with her outer looks and her inner strength. She realized that she didn't need to change herself to fit into anyone else's image of beauty. She was already complete. And more than that, she had the strength to sail through life on her own terms, independent and self-sufficient, steering her own course no matter the waters ahead.

As the boats drifted further into the distance, their soft glow fading against the night, Sanjay leaned closer to Chitra. "There's something important I want you to remember, Chitra," he said, his voice calm but firm. "Be self-sufficient. Learn to do your own work, take care of yourself independently, without relying on anyone else—not even your mother or me. You'll find a deep sense of pride in knowing that you can handle whatever comes your way on your own. Life will throw challenges, but when you're not dependent on anyone for your day-to-day needs, you'll move through those challenges with confidence."

Chitra nodded, feeling the weight of his words settle in the stillness of the evening, the illuminated boats mirroring the quiet strength she knew she needed to cultivate within herself.

"And above all, Chitra," Sanjay added, "you must be completely financially independent—the sooner, the better. That's why I've been telling you about entrepreneurship, architecture, and creating multiple streams of income. If you can control your finances, you can control your future. No one will be able to take advantage of you because you'll never be dependent on anyone."

Chitra remained silent, but she could feel the weight of her father's words. He was preparing her not just for the present but for the rest of her life. And she knew that this life experience—about being able to stand up for herself in every aspect—was one she would carry with her forever.

"There are some things," Sanjay said, his voice now softer, "that I want you to study—skills that will serve you well in life. First, study psychology. Understanding people is critical—whether in business or in your personal relationships. Emotional intelligence will help you navigate the complexities of life. It's not just about knowing what others think—it's about understanding why they think it and how to respond."

Chitra nodded, intrigued.

"Second," Sanjay continued, "work on your logical reasoning. Clear, rational thinking will help you make better decisions—whether in business or personal life. Learn to analyse situations, to think things through. It will help you avoid mistakes and navigate challenges."

Chitra listened intently, soaking in every word.

"And third," Sanjay added, "learn about finance and accounts. It's one of the most important skills you'll ever have. Saving, investing, and understanding how money works is crucial for long-term success. If you're smart about your money, you'll have the freedom to pursue your dreams without worrying about financial limitations."

Chitra smiled, seeing how her father's wisdom had guided him through life.

"Fourth," Sanjay said with a gentle smile, "practice visualization. You are a creative person. Feel the world three dimensionally. Also visualizing your goals—whether in your career, business, or personal life—helps you chart the path toward achieving them. It's not just about having dreams—it's about figuring out how to get there."

And the Fifth one, he added, "most importantly, work on your public speaking. Being able to articulate your ideas, to lead with confidence, and to inspire others is a powerful tool. Whether you're giving a presentation or leading a team, communication is key."

Chitra sat back, feeling the weight of her father's wisdom. He wasn't just talking about skills for success—he was talking about life.

Sanjay looked at Chitra with a thoughtful expression. "Chitra, as you start thinking about your future, there's something very important I want you to understand. When you're choosing your career, you have to think beyond what's exciting right now. You need to focus on something that you can do for a lifetime, something that will continue to grow with you as you grow.

"Some careers, like acting, modelling, beauty-based industries, dance, sports, or even singing, depend heavily on one's physical features or abilities. While these career paths can be highly valuable and rewarding, they are extremely short-term. As you age, your looks, physical strength, or even your voice will change or decline, and if your entire livelihood depends on these, it could become very difficult for you and your family to sustain in the long run."

"But when you choose a career based on your inner core skills, your intellect, or your expertise—things that will evolve and strengthen over time—you can build something that lasts. You'll have something you can rely on for your whole life, regardless of age or physical changes, because these are assets you can rely on throughout your life. It's about thinking long-term and finding a path that will not only bring you success today but also sustain you throughout your life."

Sanjay smiled and added, "So, when you choose your career, unlike some of your friends who may be following temporary passions, think about what you can dedicate yourself to for a lifetime. It's not just about what excites you in the moment, but about building something that will continue to support and fulfil you throughout your life."

He looked at Chitra, his eyes soft but serious. "Chitra," he continued gently, "I want you to consider architecture as a career, not because it's what I do, but because it offers the foundation to create something meaningful. Architecture isn't just about building structures—it's about understanding people, communities, and spaces. It's about creating places where lives unfold, where people can thrive."

He paused, allowing the weight of his words to settle.

"You already have an advantage," Sanjay continued. "There's a legacy here—an architectural business I've built that I want to hand over to you. It's not just a source of stability; it's a platform where you can grow, shape it in your own way, and take it to new heights. This isn't about following in my footsteps; it's about taking that foundation and making it your own."

Chitra looked at her father, her heart swelling with pride and a growing sense of responsibility.

As the evening air settled around them, Sanjay glanced at his daughter with pride. Watching her grow had been a journey filled with quiet learnings, small moments of understanding, and now the dawning realization of what her future could hold. This was more than just a conversation about career choices; it was about shaping Chitra's future as an independent thinker, an entrepreneur.

"Chitra," Sanjay began again, his voice filled with a deeper purpose, "we've talked about time, about focus, about decision-making, but there's something more important today—entrepreneurship. It's a mindset, not just a career. It's about seeing opportunities where others see obstacles. It's about never relying on just one source of income, and finding ways to create multiple streams that will keep you secure, no matter what life throws at you."

Chitra's eyes reflected the curiosity and seriousness of the life experiences her father had been sharing. Sanjay knew this moment would shape her mindset for years to come.

"Architecture," Sanjay added with a small smile, "isn't just a profession; it's a gateway. It's the foundation that allows you to think critically, solve problems, and create lasting things. But it also equips you with the entrepreneurial mindset to see beyond just one path. Once you master that, you can diversify—invest in real estate, start a design consultancy, or even follow your other passions like music or dance."

Chitra nodded, understanding the connection her father was making between her creative spirit and the practicality of architecture.

Sanjay continued, his tone soft yet filled with conviction, "I've always known you have a creative spark. I did your psychometric analysis, and it showed what I already knew—that your strengths, your way of seeing the world, are perfectly suited for architecture. Not because it's part of the family business, but because it merges creativity with practicality. That combination will give you the freedom to grow, diversify, and create other streams of income. It's about entrepreneurship, Chitra—it's about freedom."

Chitra's mind raced with possibilities. She had always thought she had to choose between being an architect, a designer, or a performer, but now her father was showing her that she could be all of them, with the right mindset.

"All those ideas I've been talking to you about over the years," Sanjay continued, his voice softening, "weren't just random pieces of advice. I've been introducing you to entrepreneurship without ever using the word. When I taught you to budget your allowance, split it between saving, spending, and giving—that was entrepreneurship. When I asked you to help make decisions in our business, those were real problems for you to solve. Even when we talked about your love for music, I asked how you could turn that passion into something sustainable."

Chitra blinked, the realization dawning on her. Her father had been guiding her toward this path all along, even when she hadn't realized it.

"And that's why architecture is the perfect fit for you," Sanjay continued, his eyes glowing with pride. "It provides a strong foundation both financially and creatively. From there, you can grow into other areas, explore different avenues, and always have the security of knowing you control your destiny."

He leaned back, watching Chitra as she processed everything. This was the moment he had been waiting for—the moment when she could see the full scope of her future.

"Remember, Chitra," Sanjay added, his voice soft but firm, "entrepreneurship means taking charge, being willing to take risks—but smart, calculated ones. It's about always keeping your long-term goals in focus and being ready to adapt."

Sanjay looked at Chitra thoughtfully and continued, "You see, Chitra, entrepreneurship isn't just about making money. It's about self-improvement, growing your knowledge, and embracing lifelong learning. The more you learn, the more you can earn. But that's only the beginning. The more you earn, the more you can help—because with success comes the ability to uplift others. And here's the beautiful part—it creates a cycle. The more you help, the happier you are.

"It's not just about financial gain, but about making a meaningful impact. True fulfilment comes from using what you've learned and earned to make a difference in the world. Learning never stops, especially in entrepreneurship. The more skills and knowledge you gain, the more opportunities you'll unlock to earn more. But earning more puts you in a position to give back, to help others, and that's where the real magic happens. The greater your impact, the greater your sense of fulfilment and happiness.

"Success, Chitra, isn't just about money. It's about how much of a difference you can make in the lives of others. That's the true reward of entrepreneurship—that's where real happiness lies."

Chitra smiled, a newfound determination sparkling in her eyes. For the first time, she saw her future not as a series of forced decisions, but as a field of endless possibilities—possibilities she had the power to create.

"Papa," she said softly, "I'll do it. I'll make sure your legacy continues."

Sanjay smiled, his heart full of pride and love. He knew that Chitra was ready. She had the tools, the life experiences, and now, the vision. And that was all she needed to become the entrepreneur he always knew she could be.

As the night deepened and the stars twinkled above them, father and daughter sat together, the weight of Sanjay's words lingering in the air. The gentle glow of the park's decorative lights mingled with the soft twinkling of stars above. Chitra was no longer just a child—she was stepping into her own future, armed with the wisdom her father had passed down to her. The world around Sanjay and Chitra had quieted, the once-bustling park now a serene landscape of shadows and warm lights. Only the occasional sound of distant laughter or the whisper of leaves in the cool breeze punctuated the stillness. The air was crisp, carrying with it the scent of blooming flowers, while the nearby lake shimmered under the reflection of the few stars that had emerged in the dark sky.

Sanjay gazed upwards for a moment, letting the peacefulness of the night wash over him before turning back to Chitra with a thoughtful smile.

"And all what I am saying are just a basic framework for you," he said softly, the warmth of his voice carrying through the stillness, "to help you with a foundation for the journey of your life. But remember, you will have to improvise. You'll have to figure things out on your own."

Chitra, her curiosity unquenched by the evening's conversation, leaned in closer. She wanted to know more, to grab every bit of the wisdom her father was sharing.

Sanjay chuckled, noticing her eagerness. "I see you're hungry for answers. But here's the thing, beta—not everything can be taught, because life doesn't work like your school, and not everything 'should' be taught, like the way your school tries you to teach. Some life experiences you'll have to learn by yourself, through experience. That's how life is. You'll stumble, you'll fail, you'll fall, but you'll have to get back up, and in the process, you'll discover who you truly are."

Chitra smiled softly, feeling the weight of her father's words settle deep within her heart.

Sanjay gazed out over the shimmering lake, the soft rustle of the trees providing a gentle backdrop to his thoughts. He turned to Chitra, her face filled with curiosity, waiting for what he would say next. After a brief pause, he began, "You know, Chitra, there's something important I've learned over the years. Sometimes in life, we stand at a crossroads, unsure which path to take. It's like that famous line from a poem I once read—'Two roads diverged in a yellow wood.'"

He smiled softly, continuing, "The point is, life presents us with choices, and we often worry about making the 'right' decision. But here's the truth: it's not about which road you take. Every path leads to experiences, and those experiences shape who you become." His words hung in the air, simple yet profound, as Chitra nodded thoughtfully, absorbing the wisdom behind them, as Sanjay continued. "At those moments, we tend to overthink, worrying about which decision is the right one. We analyse every small detail, fearing that one wrong step will change everything. But here's the truth—most of the time, it doesn't matter as much as we think it does. You see, every road we take, every choice we make, leads us forward. They're just different ways to reach the same destination. So don't overthink the small decisions. Look at the bigger picture, because, in the end, both roads will take you where you're meant to go."

He glanced at her, his eyes soft with the wisdom of experience. "Life is much bigger than those little choices. It's the big picture that matters. Sure, one path may have a few more bumps, while the other may seem smoother, but both roads lead you to where you're meant to go. So, there's no need to get stuck overthinking small decisions, whether it's which subjects to study or which friends to make. Just take a step and move forward. As long as you stay focused on your bigger goal, the rest will fall into place. What matters is how you walk the road, not which one you choose."

Chitra looked thoughtful, her father's words sinking in. "So even if I make the wrong choice sometimes, it'll still work out in the end?"

Sanjay smiled. "Exactly. It's all part of the journey. Every decision teaches you something, and that's what moves you closer to your bigger dreams. Just remember to look at the big picture and trust that you're on the right path."

And as Sanjay looked up at the sky, he felt a deep sense of contentment. His journey had been filled with life experiences, with risks and rewards, and now, he was passing that knowledge on to his daughter, knowing that she would carry it forward in her own unique way. **Together, they were building a legacy—one that would last for generations.**

ᏢᏢᏢ

My Top 10 Learnings:

1. **Discovering Passion through Reflection**: Sanjay emphasizes the importance of introspection to understand what truly drives and excites you, which is key to finding passion in your work.
2. **Balancing Personal and Professional Life**: Sanjay shares how passion in one's profession should not come at the cost of personal relationships, highlighting the need for balance between work and family.
3. **Long-term Dedication**: Finding passion in a profession is not about short-term excitement but about dedicating yourself to a path that sustains you over time.
4. **Legacy Building:** Sanjay talks about the significance of continuing the family's legacy through meaningful work that benefits future generations, creating something lasting.
5. **Entrepreneurial Mindset:** He emphasizes the importance of entrepreneurship, not just for financial gain, but for the freedom to innovate and create meaningful impact.
6. **Architecture as a Pathway:** Sanjay explains how architecture is more than just building structures; it's

about creating spaces where people live and thrive, merging creativity with practicality.

7. **Creative Freedom:** The chapter explores how finding passion in your profession gives you the creative freedom to grow and explore other interests, blending passion with practicality.

8. **Contribution to Society:** Sanjay underlines that finding passion in your profession should also include the desire to contribute positively to society, beyond personal success.

9. **Adapting Passion to Changing Circumstances:** Sanjay teaches that passion is dynamic and should be adaptable to changing circumstances, ensuring that it remains sustainable over a lifetime.

10. **Lifelong Learning:** Finally, Sanjay encourages Chitra to embrace continuous learning as a way to keep her passion alive, reminding her that learning fuels both professional success and personal growth.

5

When I Experienced Real Time Freedom

> *"I understand that carrying forward the family legacy is not just about following in your footsteps but about adding my own dreams, my own passions, and my hard work to build something even greater."*
>
> - Chitra

Chitra was growing not just in years, but in wisdom, as her father's life lessons began to resonate deeply with her. The experiences Sanjay shared were more than just stories from his past—they were guiding principles, shaping her understanding of the world and the challenges she would face. Each conversation illuminated a new facet of life, from navigating distractions and relationships to understanding true commitment and love. Through her father's words, Chitra was learning to see beyond the immediate, grasping the bigger picture of her own future, and slowly realizing the importance of these timeless lessons in her own journey ahead.

Sujata, seated nearby, had already packed up the remnants of their picnic, her calm, reassuring presence a steady anchor in the fading light of Eco Park. Her movements were slow, deliberate, as she quietly watched her husband and daughter, allowing the conversation to unfold without interference. There was something about the way Sujata moved, about the way she was always there, a quiet strength that held the family together. She wasn't just the glue that kept things running; she was the grounding force for both Sanjay and Chitra, her quiet wisdom and calm demeanour serving as a constant source of comfort.

As she sat cross-legged on the soft grass, her face bathed in the gentle glow of the park's decorative lamps, Sujata's soft smile reflected her deep understanding of the moment. She knew the importance of the words Sanjay was about to share with their daughter. They had shared conversations like this many times before, in quiet moments when life slowed down, and now, she could see the same wisdom being passed on to Chitra, who was growing up before her eyes. Tonight wasn't just about talking; it was about passing the torch of understanding from one generation to the next.

The night had settled over the park, stars twinkling faintly in the sky, casting a serene glow over the lake. The gentle rustling of leaves in the evening breeze was the only sound breaking the silence. Sanjay and Chitra, now walking away from the picnic spot, strolled slowly along the tree-lined path, taking in the beauty of the calm waters. Their steps were unhurried, their conversation rich with the wisdom Sanjay had gathered over the years. As they approached the wooden bench near the lake, the soft glow from the distant city lights reflected on the still waters, and Sanjay knew it was time to continue.

Sujata, still sitting on the grass, watched them with quiet affection, her eyes twinkling with pride and understanding. She had always admired Sanjay's way of connecting with Chitra, blending serious life lessons with a touch of humour. Tonight was no different, and she felt content knowing that Chitra was growing not just in years, but in wisdom, guided by the experiences her father was sharing.

As they sat on the bench, the conversation deepened. Sanjay glanced at Chitra, watching her absorb the beauty of the park, the calm lake, and the faint shimmer of lights. It was in these quiet moments that life's most important lessons found their way into the heart, and tonight, there was one more thought, one more piece of wisdom he wanted to share before they headed home.

Sujata's soft voice broke the stillness. "Chitra, your father is right," she said, her tone gentle but firm. "Life isn't just about following the paths laid out for you; it's about carving your own way." Her words, though few, carried weight—maternal wisdom passed down with quiet authority. "And sometimes, that's hard, but you have the strength to navigate it. You've always had it."

Her gaze softened as she looked at Chitra. "I've seen you grow, and I know you have the creativity and determination to achieve anything. But independence is key. You need to be able to rely on yourself, to take care of your own needs. It's about knowing you have the power to shape your world."

Sujata's words hung in the air, a quiet echo that carried the weight of years of experience. Her calm presence was a reflection of the life she and Sanjay had built together—one that taught their daughter not just the importance of strength, but of wisdom, resilience, and independence.

Chitra looked at her mother, feeling a deep sense of gratitude for the life experiences shared between them, lessons that would guide her long after tonight. The bond between them was unspoken, yet strong, as if the wisdom they shared formed an invisible thread tying their lives together.

Tonight marked a milestone for Chitra—it was her thirteenth birthday, a symbolic passage from childhood to something greater. Sanjay felt a sense of duty to impart his most important life experience, something that would guide her not just for the next year but for the rest of her life.

Sanjay took a deep breath, gazing at the lake where the reflection of stars shimmered. "Chitra," he began, his voice soft yet deliberate. "We've talked about many things tonight—about distractions, love, passion, and legacy. But there's something else I want you to understand before we leave."

Chitra, ever curious, tilted her head slightly, her wide eyes attentive. Her father had mentioned about time earlier, but this felt different. Sanjay seemed to be building up to something more profound, something layered and meaningful.

"This again," Sanjay said, pausing for emphasis, "is about time."

Chitra's face wrinkled in slight confusion. "Time?"

Sanjay nodded, still gazing at the shimmering lake. "Yes, time. I have told you earlier that it's the most precious thing we have, but also the thing we take for granted the most."

Chitra remained quiet, knowing from experience that her father had more to say, something important that would change the way she looked at things.

"When we're young," Sanjay continued, his voice thoughtful, "we think we have all the time in the world. We plan for the future, dream about what we'll do tomorrow, next year, someday. But what we don't often realize is that time is passing by, every single moment. And once it's gone, it's gone forever."

He paused, turning to Chitra, his eyes filled with a mix of affection and seriousness. "Time, Chitra, is life's true treasure. It's more valuable than money, more valuable than success, more valuable than anything else. Because once it's lost... you can never get it back."

Chitra's brow furrowed as she processed his words. She had always thought of time as something that just existed—always there, always moving—but never considered its fleeting nature in such stark terms.

"I didn't understand that fully when I was younger," Sanjay admitted, his voice softening as he reflected on his own life. "I mentioned this earlier, but let me share a little more. I wasted so much time, Chitra. I thought because I was young, I could afford to let days slip by. I didn't realize then that the time I was wasting was the most valuable thing I had."

He smiled, a bittersweet smile that spoke of both joy and regret. "When I was your age, I spent hours daydreaming about the future, imagining I had forever to figure things out. Even as I got older, I spent time chasing things that didn't really matter—relationships that weren't right, distractions that kept me from my goals, moments that I didn't fully appreciate."

Chitra nodded, slowly beginning to understand. The weight of her father's words felt heavier now, not just a passing thought but a life lesson rooted in his own experiences.

"And it wasn't until much later," Sanjay continued, with a quiet sadness in his voice, "that I realized how much time I had lost. Time I could never get back. That's when I learned the most important life lesson—one that I want you to learn earlier than I did: You can always earn more money, build a career, find new opportunities—but you can never regain lost time."

Chitra's eyes softened. She had always admired her father's wisdom, but hearing him speak about time this way made her see him in a new light, as someone who had learned these lessons through the trials of life.

"That's why I want you to understand this now," Sanjay said, his voice filled with urgency. "You're young, Chitra. You have so much time ahead of you, but don't waste it. Don't spend your days waiting for the future to happen because the future is happening right now. Every moment, every day, is part of your life. You need to make the most of it."

Chitra's gaze grew thoughtful. "But how do I do that, Papa? How do I make the most of my time?"

Sanjay smiled warmly, sensing the depth of her curiosity. "It's simple," he said, his tone soft but clear. "You start by being present. By appreciating the moment you're in, instead of constantly worrying about the future or regretting the past."

Sanjay leaned forward, his voice taking on a more introspective tone as he continued. "You know, Chitra, we suffer because of just two things in life—our memory and our imagination. We torture ourselves with memories of the past, replaying in our heads the moments that are already gone, things we can't change. And then, we worry about the future with our imagination, stressing over things that haven't even happened yet. But the truth is, the past no longer exists, and the future isn't here yet. Yesterday is history, tomorrow is a mystery, but today is a gift. That is why they call it the 'Present'. All we truly have is the present, this moment right now. Everything else is just nothingness, shadows of what once was or what might be."

Chitra's eyes widened, a soft "wow" escaping her lips as she absorbed the weight of her father's words. She had never thought of it like that before, and the simplicity of the truth struck her deeply. The idea that the past was gone and the future wasn't here yet, that only the present mattered, felt like a revelation. "That's... really something, Papa," she said, her voice full of admiration. "I've never thought about time like that." She sat quietly, letting the profound thought settle in.

He leaned in slightly, as if sharing a secret. "Yes. Most people spend their lives either regretting what's behind them or worrying about what's ahead. But the only time that truly matters is right now. This moment, Chitra—this is where life happens."

Chitra stayed silent, her mind turning over her father's words. She had never thought of time in such profound way, but now she saw how much of her life had been spent either looking forward to things or dwelling on the past.

"But it's not just about being present," Sanjay continued, his voice deepening as he expanded on the lesson. "It's about how you spend your time. You need to focus on things that matter—on things that bring you joy, help you grow, and make a difference in your life and the lives of others."

He softened his gaze as he looked at Chitra. "And most importantly," he added quietly, "you need to spend your time with the people you love. Because time spent with those who matter is never wasted."

Chitra's heart swelled with understanding. She had always known that time was valuable, but hearing her father speak about it like this, she realized how much of her life was still ahead—and how vital it was to use that time wisely.

As Sanjay's words hung in the evening air, rich with meaning, Chitra felt a deeper connection to the ideas he had conveyed. Time, once a distant concept, now felt real and precious. She understood that the choices she made from this moment on would shape not just her future but the value of her time—and that was the true treasure her father wanted her to cherish.

The evening air was still, the soft rustling of leaves creating a calming backdrop as Sanjay and Chitra sat together. They had covered so much ground in their conversation about life, values, and the future, but Sanjay knew there were some more life experiences that he needed to share with her. It was something simple but powerful—something that would help Chitra stay focused and make decisions in any aspect of her life.

Sanjay glanced at Chitra, her bright eyes still filled with curiosity. He smiled, feeling proud of the thoughtful young woman she was becoming.

"Chitra," Sanjay began gently, "there's a little life hack I've come up with—something I use whenever I need to make a decision or when I'm uncertain about what to do. I call it the PMF Test."

Chitra tilted her head, intrigued by the new concept. "PMF?" she repeated, unsure of what her father was about to share.

"Yes," Sanjay nodded. "It stands for Physical, Mental, and Financial. Before you decide to do anything, whether it's a small choice or a big one, I want you to ask yourself these three simple questions: Is it good for me physically? Is it good for me mentally? And is it good for me financially?"

Chitra's brow furrowed as she thought about it, trying to make sense of the acronym.

Sanjay leaned forward, his voice calm but filled with purpose. "Let's break it down. The first question—Physically. Before you do something, ask yourself, 'Is this going to help me physically? Is it going to take care of my body, my health?' If the answer is yes, then you're on the right track. If it's harmful or it'll hurt your well-being, it's a sign to rethink."

Chitra nodded. "That makes sense."

Sanjay smiled and continued, "Now the second—Mentally. This is about whether something is going to give you peace of mind or make you anxious. Will it help you grow mentally, make you happy, or is it going to drain your energy? Mental well-being is just as important as physical, if not more. You need to protect your mind, Chitra, because that's where your real strength lies."

Chitra's expression softened, and she listened intently, absorbing her father's words.

"And finally," Sanjay said, "the Financial part. Before you take any step, ask yourself, 'Is this a good decision financially? Will this add value to my life or take it away?' Now, this doesn't mean you should always focus on money. But financial decisions can impact your long-term freedom and security. It's about making sure your choices lead to stability, rather than struggle."

Chitra was quiet for a moment, processing everything. "So, if something checks all three boxes—physical, mental, and financial—it's a good choice?"

"Exactly," Sanjay nodded. "That's the essence of the PMF Test. It's a quick way to stay focused and make sure you're not led astray by short-term temptations or distractions. If something is good for you in these three aspects, then you know it's worth doing."

"But what if something is only good in two ways but not the third?" Chitra asked thoughtfully.

Sanjay smiled, appreciating her sharpness. "That's where your judgment comes in. Sometimes, you might have to balance things. For example, if a decision is great for your mental and physical health but requires some financial investment, you might decide it's worth it. But always weigh the pros and cons. The PMF Test is here to guide you, not control you."

Chitra smiled, feeling empowered by the simplicity and wisdom behind her father's words. "Thanks, Papa. I think this will really help me."

Sanjay leaned back, his heart full of pride. "It will, Chitra. This is your compass, your way of staying true to yourself. Remember—protect your body, guard your mind, and make smart financial decisions. If you can do that, you'll always find your way."

As the dusk settled deeper, casting long shadows over the lake, the soft glow of park lights flickered on, illuminating the path where Sanjay and Chitra sat. The sky, a mixture of deepening blues and oranges, seemed to reflect the quiet mood of reflection between father and daughter. Sanjay leaned back on the bench, smiling at Chitra, knowing the evening had been full of important conversations. The boats on the lake glided past, their twinkling lights casting ripples on the water, a gentle reminder of the flow of time.

Sanjay felt a sense of pride as he looked at Chitra, knowing she was already far ahead of her friends in terms of wisdom. While they might be chasing trends, worrying about fleeting things, Chitra was learning the deeper lessons of life—the kind of wisdom her peers were unlikely to be hearing at home.

Sujata, always the calm and quiet observer, had finished packing up their picnic and now sat down beside them, watching the scene unfold with a contented smile. She looked at Sanjay with that familiar look of understanding, as if she already knew what was coming.

"You know, Chitra," Sujata added, a glint of humour in her eyes, "most of your friends are still trying to figure out what they want to wear tomorrow, while you're here getting a masterclass on life experiences. Just remember, it's not a race. You're already ahead in more ways than one."

Sanjay chuckled softly at her words, grateful for Sujata's gentle way of grounding every conversation. "She's right, you know. It's not about rushing through life, but understanding it deeply. And trust me, you're already ahead. Half of what you've learned tonight will take others half of their lifetime to even begin to grasp."

Chitra smiled, a mix of pride and humility in her expression, knowing that these talks weren't just casual discussions but life lessons that would shape her future. The night air grew cooler, wrapping around them, and the soft sounds of the park in the background seemed to carry the evening forward, like the final chapter of a book yet to be written.

As they sat there together, Sanjay felt a deep sense of gratitude, not just for the wisdom he was passing on, but for the quiet strength Sujata brought to their lives. She had always been the perfect balance—serious when needed, but light and humorous at just the right moments.

"And don't forget," Sujata added, with a playful smile, "if your dad ever starts repeating himself, just remind him you've got all this figured out already."

They all laughed, the mood lightened just enough to remind them that while life's lessons were important, there was always room for joy. The deeper conversations would continue, Sanjay knew, but for now, this moment, surrounded by the quiet hum of the park and the shared bond of family, was enough.

As the dusky evening deepened into night, the faint glow of stars began to flicker in the sky, reflecting off the still waters of the lake. The atmosphere at Eco Park was serene, carrying with it the soft hum of conversations and distant laughter. Sanjay leaned back slightly on the bench, looking at Chitra with a fond smile. Tonight's discussions had already covered a lot, and though they had talked about time and life earlier, there was a different angle he wanted to touch upon now—something equally important that he had been subtly introducing to her for years: how to handle money.

"Chitra," Sanjay began, his tone steady but gentle, "I've mentioned money briefly before, but tonight, I want to go a little deeper. There are some things about finances that most people don't understand, and I wanted you to grasp them early, before you ever truly needed to. These are the lessons that shaped my approach to money, and I hope they help you too."

Chitra, curious as always, tilted her head slightly, her wide eyes attentive. Her friends often talked about money in terms of what they could buy—gadgets, clothes, trips to the mall. But Sanjay had always taught her something different, something rooted in long-term thinking. She could sense this conversation was going to expand on those earlier talks.

"First," Sanjay began, "there's income. It's what you earn—whether from a job, a business, or investments. But earning money is just the beginning. It's what you do with that income that really matters." He paused, allowing her to absorb the idea before continuing. "Many people make good money, but they're still living paycheck to paycheck because they don't understand the rest of the equation."

Chitra nodded, recalling all the times her father had emphasized the importance of looking beyond just earning money. She knew most of her friends hadn't even begun to think this way.

"Next," Sanjay continued, "are expenses. This is where people usually get it wrong. They spend everything they earn on things they think they need, but often those things don't really add any value. I've been teaching you to track your expenses, to know exactly where your money is going, and to make sure that your income is always more than your expenses. That's something most people don't learn until much later in life."

Chitra smiled, realizing how different her father's teachings were from what she heard her friends' parents say. Most focused on earning money but rarely talked about managing it well.

"And that brings me to something even more important," Sanjay said, his tone growing more serious. "It's about understanding cash flow—where your money goes and how it moves. It's not just earning more and keeping expenses controlled, but ensuring that your money is working for you, not against you."

Chitra thought about her friends always buying the latest phones or clothes, while her father had taught her to prioritize spending in ways that would benefit her in the long term.

"Now," Sanjay said, leaning forward slightly, "here's where many people fail to understand. I have told you about a difference between assets and liabilities. An asset is something that puts money into your pocket. A liability, on the other hand, takes money out of your pocket. And you need to know which is which."

He paused, watching Chitra's thoughtful expression as she absorbed the difference. "You know, Chitra, a house can be an asset if it's earning rental income. But if it's just sitting there, costing you in maintenance and mortgage payments, it's a liability. You always need to ask yourself: 'Is this going to put money into my pocket or take money out?' Most people never ask that question."

Chitra smiled, remembering the many conversations they had about what to buy and why. This was one of those moments when she realized how much she had already learned from her father's life experiences.

"And finally," Sanjay added, "we need to talk about cash flow. It's not just about how much you make but how money moves in and out of your life. If you have good cash flow—meaning more money coming in than going out—you have freedom. That's why I've taught you to invest in things that generate cash flow, like assets. The goal is to have your money work for you, not the other way around."

The night air grew cooler as they sat there, and Chitra's mind was already racing, thinking about how different this was from what her friends' parents focused on. They talked about saving or earning, but her father was teaching her how to build something lasting, how to make money grow and work for her.

Sanjay smiled softly, seeing Chitra's deepening understanding. "You see, Chitra, I've been preparing you for this for years. While your friends might focus on which job they would take when they grow up, you're already learning how to earn and manage money, invest it, and build something that will last. These are life experiences that will set you apart."

Chitra returned his smile, realizing the weight of the knowledge she had been quietly accumulating. This wasn't just about money—it was about life, about freedom, and about creating a future where she could be in control.

Sujata, who had been quietly observing from nearby, smiled warmly, proud of the deep conversations between her husband and daughter. She added with a light-hearted tone, "You're getting a head start, Chitra. Most people don't even start thinking about these things until much later."

The gentle humour from Sujata broke the seriousness of the moment, and they all shared a laugh, letting the wisdom settle in under the peaceful night sky.

As the evening deepened, casting a soft glow over the park, father and daughter sat close together, their conversation now weaving through the stillness of the night. Sujata, sitting in quiet proximity, watched them with a tender smile, her presence adding warmth to the moment. The quiet knowledge of this new tool—this wisdom about life, time, and money—bonded them even closer. Chitra realized that she had been given something precious, far beyond any material gift. It was a set of life experiences and lessons that would stay with her for life, guiding her in ways she hadn't yet fully understood. The evening air, filled with their unspoken understanding, made Chitra feel a deep sense of gratitude. She now knew that this knowledge was her foundation, one that would shape her future and always remind her of this serene evening with her parents.

"But just as I've told you about balancing time and effort," Sanjay paused, letting the weight of his words linger in the cool evening air. He turned to Chitra, his voice gentle but firm. "I also want you to think deeply about how to balance the things that come with success—like money, responsibilities, and choices. These are the things that can either empower you or overwhelm you, depending on how you handle them."

Chitra looked at him, listening intently, aware that this was another layer to the life experiences her father had been passing on all night. The soft rustling of the trees and the faint sounds from the lake seemed to underline the gravity of the moment, as Sanjay continued, "Success can give you freedom, but it also comes with its own set of challenges. You need to learn how to manage that freedom—how to make choices that will help you grow without letting the weight of responsibilities pull you down."

Sujata, observing their conversation from nearby, smiled softly. She had always admired how Sanjay balanced his wisdom with warmth, guiding Chitra with a steady hand. And now, she watched as their daughter absorbed the lessons, knowing these moments would shape her path in the years to come.

Sanjay's smile deepened as he saw Chitra's realization unfold. "And remember, as I was saying," he added, "time doesn't mean sacrificing what you love. That's why I've always believed architecture is a wonderful path for you. Not just because it's our family business, but because it will give you the freedom to live fully."

"That's where the PMF *Test* comes in," he continued. "It'll keep you grounded. Whenever you're faced with a decision—whether it's work, hobbies, or personal life—just ask yourself if it's good for you physically, mentally, and financially. If it aligns with all three, go ahead. If not, think twice."

Sanjay leaned back slightly, feeling the weight of this life tool he had passed on to his daughter, one that he was sure would guide her well into adulthood.

Chitra looked at her father, intrigued.

"Architecture," Sanjay continued, "will be one of your primary careers, but it doesn't have to take up your entire time. It's a profession that allows you to create, to think, to design—but it also gives you the flexibility and cash flow to explore your other interests, other passions. You won't be tied down to just one thing."

He paused, his voice growing softer but more resolute. "The beauty of architecture is that it allows you to build a stable financial foundation while giving you room to explore your other passions, like music or dance. You won't be tied down, Chitra. You'll be free to dream, create, and still have the mental space and the money necessary for other things that matter to you."

Once again he paused for a moment, letting the idea sink in. Chitra's mind was always buzzing with ideas—she loved music, she loved dancing, and she had shown an interest in many things beyond just the academic or professional realm. Sanjay wanted her to know that she didn't have to choose between one path or another. She could do it all.

"As I had already told you, Chitra," he continued, "one of the most amazing things about architecture is that it trains your mind to think like an entrepreneur. You learn to see the world differently, to find creative solutions, and to manage your time effectively. And because of that, you'll have the mental space and the freedom to pursue multiple streams of income, multiple vocations if you want to."

Chitra's eyes widened slightly as she took in her father's words. The idea that she could be an architect and still have time to follow her other passions—singing, dancing, or even starting her own side business—was something she hadn't considered before.

"Think of it this way," Sanjay said with a smile. "Architecture will give you a strong foundation—a profession that allows you to earn well, to create something meaningful, and to leave a legacy. But it doesn't have to consume all your time. You can use the skills you learn from architecture—time management, creativity, problem-solving—to explore other interests. You can be a singer, a dancer, or anything else you want to be."

He paused again, his voice softening. "You don't have to limit yourself, Chitra. The world is wide open for you, and with architecture as your foundation, you'll have the financial stability and the freedom to pursue whatever else you love. That's the beauty of having a career like this—you're not just tied to one thing. You're free."

Chitra smiled, her mind racing with the possibilities. She had always thought of careers as something that would demand all her time, something she would have to dedicate herself to completely. But now, her father was showing her a different way of thinking—one where she could have a stable career and still explore the other things that made her happy.

"And you'll have the time," Sanjay said softly, "you don't have to start from scratch. I've built a foundation for you—a business that you can take over, grow, and make your own. You'll gain time—time to focus on what matters to you, without having to struggle to build everything from the ground up." You'll have the freedom to build on what I've created, to make it your own, and at the same time, you'll have the flexibility to explore the things that bring you joy."

As they continued walking, the night deepening around them, Chitra felt an overwhelming sense of gratitude. Her father wasn't just passing on a business; he was giving her the freedom to craft her own life—a life where she could follow her passions, leave her mark, and spend her time wisely – he was giving her the tools to create her own path, to live a life that was both fulfilling and free. The stars twinkled above them, as if acknowledging the promise of everything that lay ahead. Chitra now understood that her future was hers to shape, with architecture as her foundation and her passions as the wings to carry her forward.

"Chitra," Sanjay said softly, his voice thoughtful yet firm, "there's something important about how we manage our time and money. You see, while time is invaluable—once it's gone, we can never get it back—money has the unique ability to help us reclaim some of that lost time. Good money allows us to buy back moments we might otherwise lose to menial tasks. If you earn well, you can delegate those tasks to others, freeing yourself up for what truly matters—the creative, meaningful things in life that give you purpose."

Chitra listened closely, nodding as she absorbed the idea.

"But here's the thing," Sanjay continued, "it's important to remember that money is just a tool. It's not the end goal. We use money to create space and time for the things that bring us joy and fulfilment. You should never chase money just for the sake of having it, but rather, see it as a way to carve your path, to focus on what matters most to you—whether it's your passions, relationships, or any greater purpose you find along the way."

His words lingered in the air as Chitra reflected on this deeper understanding of time, money, and purpose. It wasn't just about survival; it was about shaping a life that felt meaningful to her.

Sanjay leaned in, his tone a bit more serious now. "Chitra, it's not just about earning money; it's about earning enough so that you can use it to free up your time for what truly matters. When you earn well, you don't have to get bogged down by the small, repetitive tasks that eat away at your time. Instead, you can pay others to handle those things—like hiring someone to take care of household chores, administrative work, or any tasks that don't require your full creativity or attention. This way, you can focus on what really drives you—your creative projects, your passions, or even spending time with the people you love."

He paused, letting his words sink in, before continuing, "The key is to use money as a tool to buy yourself time. And that time, Chitra, is priceless. It's what allows you to think, create, innovate, and build the kind of life that's not just about surviving but thriving. Imagine being able to dedicate your energy to things that inspire you—whether it's a career that excites you or a hobby that brings you joy. That's the real power of earning well, and I want you to see money for what it truly is—a way to live a life full of purpose, without being bogged down by the day-to-day grind."

Sanjay smiled warmly as he looked at Chitra. "And that, Chitra, is the essence of true time freedom," he said. "It's not just about having more hours in the day, but about having control over how you spend those hours. When you're financially secure and can delegate tasks that don't align with your bigger goals, you're freeing yourself to focus on what truly matters. Time freedom means you get to choose—whether it's pursuing creative passions, spending meaningful moments with family, or simply reflecting on life. It's about using the time you've earned, through hard work and smart decisions, to build a life that you love and that brings you fulfilment."

He paused for a moment, then added thoughtfully, "Remember, money is just a means to an end. It's not about having more for the sake of it, but about using it wisely to gain the freedom to live life on your terms."

The night deepened and the hum of Eco Park quieted and Sanjay's thoughts focused towards the subject close to his heart—the family business that had shaped much of his life. Looking at Chitra, now stepping into adolescence, he felt a deep responsibility to impart the significance of the legacy she would one day inherit. There was something profound about continuing a family's business legacy, something that went beyond financial gain. It was about pride, identity, and the strength of building something that could stand the test of time.

"Chitra," he said softly, his voice carrying the weight of years of experience, "our family business isn't just a company—it's our story. It's what I've built not just for myself, but for you. And now, you're not just my daughter—you're the princess of this business empire. You've been placed on a high pedestal that many never get the chance to stand on. But it's important to understand that the higher the pedestal, the more you can see and grow."

Chitra, ever curious, listened intently, her father's words stirring something deeper in her.

"You see," Sanjay continued, "I've worked hard to build this platform for you, so you wouldn't have to start from scratch. That's the beauty of a family business—it's a pyramid, with each generation building upon the work of the previous one. I've spent years laying the foundation, and now, you're already standing on a strong base. But it's not just about maintaining what we have—it's about expanding, about taking the legacy to new heights."

He paused, letting the idea settle. "You don't need to worry about where to begin. I've already lifted you to a place where your vision can expand beyond what I could have imagined. Your role now, as you step into the family business, is to continue building—to grow it, diversify it, and add your unique touch. What you do will not just reflect on the business—it will shape the future of our family's legacy for generations to come."

Chitra smiled faintly, understanding the weight and privilege of the responsibility her father was speaking about. She had always known the business was important, but now, Sanjay was framing it as more than a job or a career—it was her inheritance, her chance to make a lasting mark on the world, standing on a foundation that had been meticulously built for her.

"Think of it this way," Sanjay said, his voice growing more animated. "You're starting from a higher place than most. And from this vantage point, you can see further, reach higher, and dream bigger. You have the opportunity to innovate, to expand, and to take what I've started into new directions. But remember, with that privilege comes the responsibility of making sure the legacy grows, that it thrives, and that it remains strong for the generations that will come after you."

Chitra looked up at her father, her mind racing with possibilities, but also with a growing sense of pride. She wasn't just inheriting a business—she was inheriting a dream, one that had been built with love, sacrifice, and vision.

"And that," Sanjay added with a smile, "is the true power of continuing a family legacy. You're not just preserving something—you're shaping the future, using everything I've built to create something even greater."

Sanjay felt a deep sense of peace as they walked together. He had shared with his daughter not only the life experiences he had learned through his own life but also the gift of time and freedom. And he knew that Chitra would carry these life experiences with her, using them to build a future that was uniquely her own—a future where she could be an architect, an entrepreneur, a creator, and anything else she chose to be.

The stars above twinkled brightly as if to echo the promise of all that lay ahead, and in that moment, Sanjay knew that Chitra would step into her future with confidence, guided by the wisdom he had shared and the freedom she had been given.

As they started walking towards the exit gate of quiet park, the rustle of leaves underfoot and the soft glow of street lamps lighting their way, Chitra felt the weight of her father's words sink in deeper. But with that weight came excitement. She was ready—not just to carry forward her father's legacy but to create her own path. She was determined to make her family proud, to uphold the name her parents had worked so hard to establish.

Sujata, walking beside them with her calm grace, glanced at Chitra with a knowing smile. "You know, Chitra," she said in her gentle voice, "your father has shared a lot of wisdom tonight, but don't forget—it's not just about the big things. It's also about the small habits. Like maybe starting with keeping your room organized? Your books and toys aren't going to arrange themselves."

Chitra grinned, her excitement bubbling over into a playful response. "Oh, don't worry, Mamma. I'll arrange my books just like Papa taught me to manage assets—carefully and strategically."

Sanjay chuckled, his voice filled with warmth. "Just make sure you don't misplace the 'assets' like you had misplaced your school notebook yesterday."

Chitra laughed, lightening the mood. "If I can master organizing my books and toys, maybe I'm halfway to running an empire!"

Sujata joined in with a soft laugh, her tone teasing yet affectionate. "Well, let's hope your empire has fewer misplaced textbooks."

The banter continued while they walked towards the parking zone, and the light-heartedness eased the intensity of the conversations they had shared earlier. As they prepared to head home, the city lights of Kolkata flickered in the distance, a reminder of the bustling world awaiting them.

For Chitra, the journey home was filled with reflection. Her father's words weren't just lessons; they were the foundation for her future. With her parents by her side, guiding her with wisdom, humour, and unwavering support, she felt confident—ready to face the world.

And as the night deepened, Chitra felt a quiet sense of resolve settle within her. She knew she was ready to carry the family name forward, and to make her own unique mark on the world. She was determined to honour the legacy of their family, but also to take it to new heights, shaping it with her own vision and drive. The path ahead was challenging, but with her parents' guidance and her own growing sense of purpose, she felt more prepared than ever to face it. **The future belonged to her—and so did the legacy of the Chakrabarti Family!**

ppp

My Top 10 Learnings:

1. **Time Freedom is Priceless:** Sanjay explains to Chitra that real freedom comes when you can control your time. Money can buy back time by allowing you to delegate tasks and focus on what truly matters in life.
2. **Money is a Tool, Not the Goal:** The essence of earning well is not just to accumulate wealth, but to use it as a tool to gain time freedom and pursue personal passions and meaningful endeavours lifelong.
3. **Focus on What Matters:** True success isn't just about financial gain but about having the time and freedom to focus on things that inspire you, like creative projects, family, or hobbies.
4. **Balance Work and Life:** Sanjay highlights the importance of balancing financial success with time for personal interests, explaining that you don't have to sacrifice one for the other if managed well.
5. **Delegate the Small Tasks:** A major point is the value of outsourcing routine, time-consuming tasks to free up energy and focus for higher-level thinking, creativity, and personal growth.
6. **Live Life with Purpose:** Sanjay emphasizes that time freedom allows you to live a life of purpose, creating,

innovating, and thriving rather than just surviving.

7. **Success is About Choice:** Having financial security gives you the choice of how to spend your time, whether that's pursuing passions or spending quality time with loved ones.

8. **The Importance of Smart Financial Management:** Sanjay reminds Chitra that smart money management and investments, like cash flow assets, are key to achieving time freedom and avoiding being bogged down by the grind.

9. **True Fulfilment Comes from Helping Others:** Sanjay points out that financial success also gives you the means to help others, which in turn brings personal fulfilment and happiness.

10. **Architect Your Own Life:** Sanjay encourages Chitra to think of her future career as a foundation that provides stability and time freedom, allowing her to pursue other interests like dancing or travel without being tied down completely.

My Letter To Your Mother

My Dearest Sujata,

As I sit here, far from home on another new assignment, my thoughts continuously drift back to you and Chitra. Even though I'm not physically there, my heart remains forever connected to you both. The love we share is much deeper than distance, and I know you will continue to guide Chitra with the same grace, wisdom, and strength you've always shown.

First and foremost, I want to thank you. You've been the steady foundation of our family, balancing an incredible career with the demands of our home. From the day I met you—such an ambitious and driven young girl—to now, as the CEO of one of West Bengal's most respected healthcare chains, you've grown into someone who never ceases to amaze me. And yet, through all your success, you never let Chitra or me feel neglected. You've always been present, showing Chitra through your actions what it means to be a strong and capable woman. I admire you more than words can express.

Chitra is entering a new chapter in her life, and I know she will face moments of uncertainty. But she has us, and most importantly, she has you—her anchor, her guide. You've always been her role model, and I trust you will continue to reinforce the values we both hold dear as she steps into adulthood.

One of the most valuable life experiences I want Chitra to learn is the importance of patience, especially when it comes to love and relationships. People rush into things these days, but true love, real companionship—it takes time. Chitra doesn't need to jump into relationships just because her friends are doing the same. I know that you too want her to wait for someone who truly understands and values her. A partner who will respect her heart, her dreams, and her ambitions, just as we've taught her to respect herself.

Marriage, as we both know, is more than just a union of two people; it's the joining of two families, histories, and values. You, Sujata, have always been exceptional in navigating these dynamics. Whether it was managing both of our parents' expectations or balancing your career with our home, you've done it all with such grace. This is something I hope Chitra learns from you—the importance of choosing a partner who not only loves her but respects her *family and the legacy she carries.*

Our family names are more than just our religion or identity, because they carry centuries of tradition, wisdom, and responsibility. By marrying into a similar heritage, Chitra will be continuing that legacy, ensuring that the values we've cherished are passed down to future generations. It's not about discrimination, but about continuity. It's about preserving the principles that have shaped us for centuries.

Sujata, you've shown me that true love is not about some instant passion or romantic gestures. It's about building something lasting, something that endures against all odds. And that's the experience I want Chitra to take with her when she chooses her life partner. She must understand that her heart, mind, and future are all intertwined, and she must wait until she finds someone worthy of her.

As Chitra steps into her teenage years, I know she'll face many choices. I have offered her a framework—a set of values and ideas to guide her through life. And I know that you are the best person to remind and reinforce these concepts, over and over again as she grows up.

Chitra must understand the power of personal responsibility—she controls her own destiny. Life will present both challenges and opportunities, but she must take charge of her decisions, whether in her career, relationships, or personal growth. No one can define her worth except herself. She also needs to invest in long-term value, be it education, business, or relationships. These are the foundations that will serve her throughout life.

Time, Sujata, is far more precious than money—once lost, it can never be regained. I hope that Chitra, as she grows, understands this. I want her to spend her time wisely, on the things that truly matter most in her life, and in her career. Then there's another truth, my love: while time is invaluable, good money allows us to buy back some of that time. Earning well means being able to delegate the menial tasks to others, freeing up space to do the creative and meaningful things in life. It's about using money as a tool, not a goal—so that Chitra can carve her career path, focusing on what brings her purpose, not just survival.

Speaking of her career, I know we've talked a lot about architecture. It's not just a family business—it's a pathway to financial independence and freedom. Architecture will allow Chitra to build a legacy, while also giving her the flexibility and the cash flow required to pursue other personal interests. She's not starting from scratch; I've laid the foundation for her. This will give her the time, space and money to explore other ventures, whether it's music, dance, or something else entirely. I've always encouraged multiple streams of income, and I want her to understand the importance of diversifying her financial stability.

Chitra should focus on developing key skills like understanding people, just as you've always excelled at, Sujata. Your empathy and listening abilities are qualities I hope she inherits, as they will benefit her in both personal relationships and business. Financial literacy is also crucial—she must learn to manage money, invest wisely, save, and spend thoughtfully, giving her the independence and freedom she needs. Above all, strong communication will be invaluable, whether in a professional setting or personal conversations. You've always been excellent at this, and I trust you'll help her refine these abilities too.

Sujata, I know you'll guide Chitra with the same love and wisdom you've always shown. She has inherited your strength, your grace, and your intelligence. I have no doubt she will grow into the extraordinary woman we both dream of her becoming.

Thank you, my love, for being my partner in everything. For giving me more than I could ever ask for. Even while I'm away, I know you'll continue to lead Chitra with love and strength. She is a reflection of you in so many ways, and I'm incredibly proud of both of you.

With all my love,

Sanjay

Epilogue

As you reach the epilogue of this fictional journey of *Give Me Back My Time*, it's important to reflect on the wisdom shared by Sanjay with his daughter, Chitra.

This book, structured around life lessons drawn from personal experiences, serves as both a father's heartfelt message to his daughter and a guide for anyone navigating life's complex choices. The dialogue focuses on time management, family legacy, entrepreneurship, and personal growth, and how these principles apply to living a meaningful and fulfilling life. Here's a breakdown of essential learnings from each chapter:

Chapter 1: When I Learned Life's First Secrets

In the first chapter, Sanjay reflects on the early lessons of life, primarily cantered on time, family, and personal growth. He shares with Chitra how the foundation of success is laid during the formative years and that mistakes along the way are learning opportunities. The message is to value time, cherish family, and embrace growth.

> *"Time, Chitra, is like sand slipping through your fingers—once it's gone, you can't get it back."*

> *"The world won't always revolve around you; learning to share your*

> ***time and love with others is part of growing up."***

> **"Every mistake is a lesson in disguise, and if you learn from it, you've turned it into something valuable."**

Sanjay's reflections in this chapter centre around understanding life's fundamental truths, particularly in adolescence. Key takeaways are:

1. **Time is Finite in your Life:** Sanjay emphasizes the importance of valuing time. It is a non-renewable resource, because our days are numbered, and using it wisely from a young age sets the foundation for future success.

2. **Focus on What Matters:** The distractions of youth, such as peer pressure and trivial pursuits, can often lead us off course. Sanjay advises focusing on long-term goals and values.

3. **Learning from Mistakes:** Mistakes are inevitable, but it's crucial to view them as opportunities for growth rather than setbacks.

4. **The Role of Family:** The chapter highlights how family can be a guiding force, providing both support and wisdom to steer through life's challenges.

5. **Self-Reflection:** Sanjay encourages Chitra to regularly reflect on her experiences, suggesting that personal growth begins with self-awareness.

Chapter 2: When I Moved On From Distractions to Clarity

This chapter focuses on how Sanjay moved beyond the distractions of his youth to find clarity and purpose. He encourages Chitra to stay focused on her long-term goals and not be swayed by temporary pleasures or social pressures.

> *"Distractions will always be there, but clarity comes when you learn to say no to what doesn't serve your purpose."*

> *"True focus is about cutting out the noise and honing in on what really matters in the long run."*

> *"It's not the easiest road that leads to success, but the one where you walk with intention and discipline."*

This chapter focuses on moving from distractions to finding clarity in purpose and direction. Key lessons include:

1. **Clearing the Clutter:** Sanjay advises that removing distractions—whether physical, mental, or financial—creates space for true focus and productivity.
2. **Defining Purpose:** Once distractions are eliminated, the next step is to define one's purpose. Sanjay talks about the importance of knowing why you are pursuing a particular path.
3. **The Power of Discipline:** Clarity only comes with consistent effort and discipline. Without daily habits that align with your goals, even the best-laid plans can fall apart.
4. **Setting Priorities:** Sanjay explains that to make progress, it's crucial to prioritize tasks that bring you closer to your life's goals.
5. **Time Management:** The discipline of managing one's time effectively is central to this chapter. Sanjay highlights the importance of allocating time to things that matter most.

Chapter 3: When I Discovered the True Meaning of Love

In this chapter, Sanjay reflects on love, explaining to Chitra that true love goes far beyond superficial attraction. It's about continuous commitment, support, and growing together through life's challenges. The chapter delves into his relationship with Sujata and the lessons learned from their journey.

"Love is a choice you make every

single day—it's not just about your instant feelings, but about standing by someone through thick and thin."

"The truest form of love is not when everything is perfect, but when you're able to grow together through the imperfections."

"Real love doesn't try to change you; it helps you become the best version of yourself."

Sanjay talks about relationships, emphasizing the significance of understanding the deeper meanings of love and commitment. The core learnings are:

1. **Love Is a Daily Choice:** Rather than seeing love as an uncontrollable force, Sanjay discusses how love is a conscious decision, especially in long-term commitments.

2. **Mutual Support:** Successful relationships are built on mutual support, where each partner strengthens the other through challenges.

3. **Communication Is Key:** Open, honest, and thoughtful communication forms the bedrock of strong relationships. Misunderstandings are often the result of poor communication.

4. **Self-Love:** Sanjay stresses that to love someone else fully, one must first develop a strong sense of self-love and self-worth.

5. **Growth Together:** Relationships should foster growth. The best partnerships are those where both individuals evolve together rather than stagnate.

Chapter 4: Where I Found Passion in My Profession

Here, Sanjay discusses how he discovered passion in his profession as an entrepreneur and architect, encouraging Chitra to align her career with her passions. He stresses the importance of finding joy in work and pursuing a path that fulfils both personal and professional ambitions.

> *"A career should be more than a paycheck—it should be a reflection of your passions and purpose."*

> *"True passion in your work means finding joy in the process, not just the results."*

"Your job isn't just what you do, Chitra—it's who you become through the works you choose to do everyday."

Sanjay reflects on his career journey, offering insights into discovering passion in one's work. The essential lessons include:

1. **Aligning Passion with Profession:** True success comes when you find a profession that aligns with your core passion. For Sanjay, entrepreneurship and architecture wasn't just about a job; it was his inner calling, his gathered wisdom, his strength.

2. **Long-Term Vision:** Sanjay encourages Chitra to choose a career path that offers growth and fulfilment over the long term, not just in the immediate future.

3. **Learning Never Stops:** Lifelong learning is critical for staying relevant and passionate in your profession. Sanjay emphasizes that even after years of experience, there is always more to learn.

4. **Creating Impact:** A meaningful profession isn't just about personal success; it's about contributing to the broader community. Sanjay reflects on how his work has positively impacted others.

5. **Enjoying the Process:** Passion for your profession means enjoying the daily grind as much as the final results. Sanjay talks about the satisfaction that comes from immersing oneself in meaningful work.

Chapter 5: When I Experienced Real Time Freedom

In this final chapter, Sanjay talks about achieving real time freedom through financial independence and smart choices. He explains that success isn't about wealth alone, but about having the freedom to spend time on what truly matters—family, passions, and personal fulfilment.

- *"Money is a tool, Chitra—use it to buy back your time, not to tie yourself down."*

- *"True freedom isn't about having more money; it's about having more time to do what brings you joy."*

- *"Success, in the end, isn't measured by what you earn, but by the freedom you have to live your life on your own terms."*

This chapter explores the concept of time freedom and how financial independence ties into it. The critical takeaways are:

1. **Earning for Freedom:** Sanjay explains that money should be viewed as a tool for buying time. The ultimate

goal is not wealth itself, but the freedom to spend time on what truly matters.

2. **Delegating Tasks:** By earning well, one can delegate menial tasks and focus on high-impact activities. This allows for better time management and less burnout.

3. **Creating Passive Income:** Sanjay advises investing in assets that generate income, freeing up time to pursue personal passions and hobbies.

4. **Freedom to Explore Interests:** Financial independence provides the luxury of time to explore interests outside of work, such as travel, hobbies, and spending quality time with family.

5. **Balance Between Work and Life:** Sanjay underscores the importance of achieving a balance between professional success and personal fulfilment, ensuring that neither is sacrificed.

These chapters are tied together by a central theme: the importance of making thoughtful choices that prioritize long-term fulfilment, personal growth, and meaningful relationships. Sanjay's advice to Chitra is timeless, offering her a path to navigate life with intention and purpose.

In Give Me Back My Time, Sanjay's conversations with Chitra offer timeless wisdom on navigating life's complexities. From the importance of managing time and money to the deeper meanings of love, relationships, entrepreneurship, and career fulfilment, the book serves as a roadmap for teenagers stepping into adulthood. Each chapter builds on the lessons of the previous one, culminating in a philosophy that emphasizes long-term thinking, personal growth, and the importance of contributing to the world around you.

Sanjay's final message is clear: **Life is a series of choices which we make everyday. Each decision shapes our future, and with careful thought, discipline, and love, we can carve out a life of meaning and purpose.**

Some Books Which You Must Read

Rich Dad Poor Dad

"Rich Dad Poor Dad is a 1997 book written by Robert T. Kiyosaki and Sharon Lechter. It advocates the importance of financial literacy, financial independence and building wealth through investing in assets, real estate investing, starting and owning businesses, as well as increasing one's financial intelligence."

Men Are from Mars, Women Are from Venus

"Men Are from Mars, Women Are from Venus is a book written by American author and relationship counselor John Gray. One of the key messages that Gray discusses is that men and women have to understand and respect our differences. By doing that, our relationships can improve. Throughout the book he shares how men and women communicate differently."

Inner Engineering: A Yogi's Guide to Joy

"*Inner Engineering: A Yogi's Guide to Joy is a 2016 book written by Indian yogi and mystic Sadhguru. The book was featured among The New York Times Best Seller in the spirituality and self-help category for November 2016.*"

Boundaries: When to Say Yes, How to Say No, to Take Control of Your Life

"Boundaries: When to Say Yes, How to Say No, to Take Control of Your Life by Dr. Henry Cloud and Dr. John Townsend makes the case that if a person doesn't set and establish and hold strong boundaries for themselves, then bad things will happen. Boundaries define us. They define what is me and what is not me. A boundary shows us where I end and someone else begins, leading us to a sense of ownership. We must have physical boundaries (the wisdom to determine who may touch us and under what circumstances), mental boundaries (the freedom to express our own thoughts and opinions) and emotional boundaries (the ability to manage our own feelings and disengage from the manipulative emotions of others)."

The Teenager's Guide to Life, the Universe and Being Awesome: Super-Charge Your Life

"This book by Andrew Cope is a reminder that as a teenager you are awesome and a prompt for bigger and better things. It asks not what you want from life, but what kind of person you want to be, exposing the key to planning for your future - building your best qualities so you can stand out and live a brilliant, energetic, successful life."

Think and Grow Rich

"Think and Grow Rich is a book written by Napoleon Hill and Rosa Lee Beeland released in 1937 and promoted as a personal development and self-improvement book. He claimed to be inspired by a suggestion from business magnate and later-philanthropist Andrew Carnegie."

12 Rules for Life: An Antidote to Chaos

"12 Rules for Life: An Antidote to Chaos is a 2018 self-help book by the Canadian clinical psychologist Jordan Peterson. It provides life advice through essays in abstract ethical principles, psychology, mythology, religion, and personal anecdotes."

The Little Book of Yes: How to win friends, boost your confidence and persuade others

"*The Little Book of Yes: How to Win Friends, Boost your Confidence and Persuade Others by Noah Goldstein, Steve Martin and Robert Cialdini is a described as a "travel-sized handbook" and contains 21 different persuasion techniques. Most techniques are written up in just 6 pages so you can quickly dip in and out of the book as necessary.*"

Attitude is Everything

"*Jeff Keller has put together a well written, insightful book to introduce anyone to the science and application of a positive mental attitude. IF YOU CAN DREAM IT, YOU CAN DO IT! Do you dread going to work? Do you feel tired, unhappy, weighed down? Have you given up on your dreams? The foremost objective of the book is to make you believe that you can achieve anything you desire, because positive thinking and sound visualization ability can shift things in our favour.*"

The Secret

"*The Secret is a 2006 self-help book by Rhonda Byrne, based on the earlier film of the same name. It is based on the belief of the pseudoscientific law of attraction, which claims that thought alone can influence objective circumstances within one's life. The book alleges energy as assurance of its*" *effectiveness.*"

www.ingramcontent.com/pod-product-compliance
Lightning Source LLC
Chambersburg PA
CBHW021541150726
47990CB00006B/2340